Asia Bible Commentary Series

ESTHER

Langham
GLOBAL LIBRARY

For many Christians, reading Esther is like entering a strange new land. Here is a book unlike any other in the Bible. But with Peter Lau's careful reading of the text to hand, they have a guide that will not only help them to find their way around, they will understand the ways in which this book continues to speak into contemporary life. A helpful guide, Lau attends carefully both to the context of the text and the experience of reading Esther in Asia today, showing how these two enrich our discipleship.

Rev David G. Firth, PhD
Old Testament Tutor and Academic Dean,
Trinity College, Bristol, UK

This excellent commentary skillfully combines knowledge of the literary devices at work in the book of Esther, and knowledge of the cultural background from which the book was written, with a careful study of the text. The results of this process are applied specifically to the Asian context and written in language that a layman can understand. Without presenting literary analysis, exegesis, and application in different sections, as in many commentaries, this commentary exhibits a rare combined approach. It demonstrates the kind of integration which I hope will be the hallmark of contemporary Asian biblical and theological scholarship. The Bible is an integrated book and it is good for Bible commentaries also to reflect this integration.

Ajith Fernando, DD
Teaching Director, Youth for Christ, Sri Lanka

Asia Bible Commentary Series

ESTHER

Peter H. W. Lau

General Editor
Federico G. Villanueva

Old Testament Consulting Editors
Yohanna Katanacho, Tim Meadowcroft, Joseph Shao

New Testament Consulting Editors
Steve Chang, Andrew Spurgeon, Brian Wintle

© 2018 Peter H. W. Lau

Published 2018 by Langham Global Library
An imprint of Langham Publishing
www.langhampublishing.org

Langham Publishing and its imprints are a ministry of Langham Partnership

Langham Partnership
PO Box 296, Carlisle, Cumbria CA3 9WZ, UK
www.langham.org

Published in partnership with Asia Theological Association

ATA
QCC PO Box 1454 – 1154, Manila, Philippines
www.ataasia.com

ISBNs:
978-1-78368-505-9 Print
978-1-78368-506-6 ePub
978-1-78368-508-0 PDF

British Library Cataloguing in Publication Data
A catalogue record for this book is available from the British Library

ISBN: 978-1-78368-505-9

Cover & Book Design: projectluz.com

To Kathryn –
My companion
Who nudges me on
Even when God is hidden.

CONTENTS

Commentary

Topics

SERIES PREFACE

In recent years, we have witnessed one of the greatest shifts in the history of world Christianity. It used to be that the majority of Christians lived in the West, but Christians are now evenly distributed around the globe. This shift has implications for the task of interpreting the Bible from within our respective contexts, which is in line with the growing realization that every theology is contextual. The questions that we bring into our reading of the Bible will be shaped by our present realities as well as our historical and social locations. There is a need therefore to interpret the Bible for our own contexts.

The Asia Bible Commentary Series addresses this need. In line with the mission of the Asia Theological Association Publications, we have gathered Asian evangelical Bible scholars to write commentaries on each book of the Bible. The mission is to "produce resources that are biblical, pastoral, contextual, missional, and prophetic for pastors, Christian leaders, cross-cultural workers, and students in Asia." Although the Bible can be studied for different reasons, we believe that it is given primarily for the edification of the Body of Christ (2 Tim 3:16–17). The ABCS is designed to help pastors in their sermon preparation, cell group leaders or lay leaders in their Bible study groups, and those training in seminaries or Bible Schools.

Each commentary begins with an introduction that provides general information about the book's author and original context, summarizes the main message or theme of the book, and outlines its potential relevance to a particular Asian context. The introduction is followed by an exposition that combines exegesis and application. Here, we seek to speak to and empower Christians in Asia by using our own stories, parables, poems, and other cultural resources as we expound the Bible.

The Bible is actually Asian in that it comes from ancient West Asia, and there are many similarities between the world of the Bible and traditional Asian cultures. But there are also many differences that we need to explore in some depth. That is why the commentaries also include articles or topics in which we bring specific issues in Asian church, social, and religious contexts into dialogue with relevant issues in the Bible. We do not seek to resolve every tension that emerges but rather to allow the text to illumine the context and vice versa.

May the Holy Spirit, who inspired the writers of the Bible, bring light to the hearts and minds of all who use these materials, to the glory of God and to the building up of the churches!

Federico G. Villanueva

General Editor

AUTHOR'S PREFACE

In my experience, the book of Esther is not a church favorite. I have attended churches in four continents over four decades, but I cannot recall studying it in a small group. Of the thousands of sermons I've heard, I cannot clearly recall any on Esther, although there may have been a one-off Esther sermon somewhere in my dim past. So I was delighted to have the chance to study this book in preparation for writing this commentary.

What I discovered was that hearers found the book of Esther engaging and applicable. After hearing a sermon on Esther people would often say to me, "You make the narrative so interesting!" I would reply in all honesty, "No! I am just bringing out the excitement and interest that are already in the narrative." After preaching different series of sermons on Esther among people from various ethnic and church backgrounds, I'm convinced that God's word is living and active. Its blade remains razor sharp, it still divides "soul and spirit, joints and marrow; it judges the thoughts and attitudes of the heart" (Heb 4:12).

And the sad part: some of us as Christians have been depriving ourselves of the richness and power of God's word by not engaging with neglected books of the Bible such as Esther. For although it was written by someone a long time ago, in a place away from most of us (those in West Asia excepted), its ultimate author is God. He does not change. His truth does not change. He revealed more of himself and his truth as time went on (in the Old Testament and especially in Christ and the New Testament), but "*All Scripture* is God-breathed and is useful for teaching, rebuking, correcting and training in righteousness, so that the servant of God may be thoroughly equipped for every good work" (2 Tim 3:16–17). We would do well to grasp hold of all of Scripture.

Writing can be a lonely task, but I thank all of those who have made it much less so for me. Thank you to my wife Kathryn, who is and has been my first and best sermon hearer from the day we got married. Thank you to all the congregation members and those in the seminary community who endured different versions of my Esther sermons. Your facial expressions while I preached, and your probing questions afterwards, helped me to clarify and correct my thinking. I thank those who suggested other and better illustrations and applications for passages. Alert readers will notice that the sermon DNA remains. Thank you also to the participants in my Ruth and Esther elective at Seminari Theoloji Malaysia, who raised many interesting issues as we waded through the narrative together. You have all contributed to my thinking on Esther.

Thanks also to Steven, Davin and Daniel, who provided feedback on earlier drafts of this commentary and/or my Esther conference paper. Thank you to Ruth Wong, my "in-house" proof reader, and to Anne C. Harper, ATA's guest editor. Thank you to Havilah Dharamraj and Rico Villanueva for showing me the ropes as I began writing this commentary, and for providing helpful Asian contextual insights.

This commentary is my – or perhaps I should say *our* – humble contribution to bringing God's word to life in the hearts and minds of his people. Foremost, for those of us in Asia, but also for the rest of God's world – all seven continents included. To the praise of his glorious grace!

Peter H. W. Lau

LIST OF ABBREVIATIONS

BOOKS OF THE BIBLE

Old Testament

Gen, Exod, Lev, Num, Deut, Josh, Judg, Ruth, 1–2 Sam, 1–2 Kgs, 1–2 Chr, Ezra, Neh, Esth, Job, Ps/Pss, Prov, Eccl, Song, Isa, Jer, Lam, Ezek, Dan, Hos, Joel, Amos, Obad, Jonah, Mic, Nah, Hab, Zeph, Hag, Zech, Mal

New Testament

Matt, Mark, Luke, John, Acts, Rom, 1–2 Cor, Gal, Eph, Phil, Col, 1–2 Thess, 1–2 Tim, Titus, Phlm, Heb, Jas, 1–2 Pet, 1–2–3 John, Jude, Rev

BIBLE TEXTS AND VERSIONS

Divisions of the canon

NT	New Testament
OT	Old Testament

Ancient texts and versions

AT	Alpha Text
LXX	Septuagint
MT	Masoretic Text

Modern versions

ESV	English Standard Version
NASB	New American Standard Bible
NET	New English Translation
NIV	New International Version
NJPS	Tanakh: The Holy Scriptures: The New JPS Translation
NKJV	New King James Version
NRSV	New Revised Standard Version

Journals, reference works, and series

AB	Anchor Bible
ABCS	Asia Bible Commentary Series
ABD	*Anchor Bible Dictionary*
BBR	*Bulletin for Biblical Research*
BDB	*Brown-Driver-Briggs Hebrew and English Lexicon of the OT*
Bib	*Biblica*
BST	Bible Speaks Today
EvQ	*Evangelical Quarterly*
HALOT	*Hebrew and Aramaic Lexicon of the Old Testament*
JBL	*Journal of Biblical Literature*
JSOT	*Journal for the Study of the Old Testament*
JSOTSup	Journal for the Study of the Old Testament Supplement Series
NCBC	New Century Bible Commentary
NIVAC	New International Version Application Commentary
NSBT	New Studies in Biblical Theology
OTL	Old Testament Library
SBLDS	Society of Biblical Literature Dissertation Series
TOTC	Tyndale Old Testament Commentaries
VT	*Vetus Testamentum*
WBC	Word Biblical Commentary

INTRODUCTION

The experience of reading the book of Esther might be like my experience of visiting Siem Reap, Cambodia. On first impression, the city had a vaguely familiar feel to other Southeast Asian cities I had previously visited: the people looked similar, they ate rice and noodles, and bargaining was expected at markets. However, on further exploration, the situation became more unfamiliar. As I entered the Angkor Archaeological Park and wandered around the monuments, buildings, and the ruins, I was transported to a strange, exotic, faraway place. At Angkor Wat, the grand temple complex built in the twelfth century, I needed a tour guide to explain the significance of what I was seeing, such as the layout, architecture and the meaning of the many bas-reliefs, especially those with religious figures depicting narratives and myths. Visits to multiple sites in the Archaeological Park helped me identify and become more familiar with repeated ideas and themes. Yet it was the Angkor National Museum – my starting point – that helped me understand how the temples and buildings fit into the history of the Angkor Empire and that gave me insights into this vast empire from centuries before.

Esther is a strange book. On first reading, some customs and ideas are familiar. We may have heard the names of some of the main characters. At least most of us know the book is found somewhere in the Old Testament. However, as we start to read it, we may find that some customs are a bit odd. We may find that the actions of the characters are unexpected and even shocking. We may become disorientated by this exotic, faraway place, and we may not be able to place it within the broader storyline of the Bible. Further, it is peculiar for a book in the Bible not to mention God anywhere in the whole narrative!

This commentary is like a tour guide. It provides background information and explanations as we explore the book of Esther. However, before we step into the Esther narrative, we must visit the "museum" for an introduction. This prepares us for how the tour guide approaches our visit and explains why the book includes certain information. For this commentary not only takes us into a strange land, but it also helps us to bring the information back home – to help us live in the here and now. We bring back not only history but also theology and ethics.

The following introduction begins with "Reading Esther in Persia," which outlines the historical context and helps us understand how the book of Esther would have been understood by the original audience. The introduction continues with "Reading Esther in the Canon," which provides the Scriptural context for us to understand Esther. It then finishes with "Reading Esther in Asia," which outlines the main themes of the book and their relevance for us today.

READING ESTHER IN PERSIA

The Esther narrative was set in the capital city Susa during the reign of the Persian Empire. It was the great world empire after the Babylonian Empire (539 BC) until it fell to the Greek Empire under Alexander the Great (333 BC). The king in the Esther narrative was Xerxes (1:1), who reigned from 486–465 BC. He succeeded his father Darius I (reigned 522–486 BC), during whose reign the rebuilding of the Jerusalem Temple was completed (Hag 2:1–9; Ezra 6:15; 516 BC). His predecessors were Cambyses II (530–522 BC) and Cyrus (559–530 BC), under whom the exiles were allowed to return to rebuild Jerusalem (539 BC; 2 Chr 36:22–23; Ezra 1:1–4). Most Jews remained in the diaspora, however, including the main Jewish characters in the Esther narrative – Esther and Mordecai.

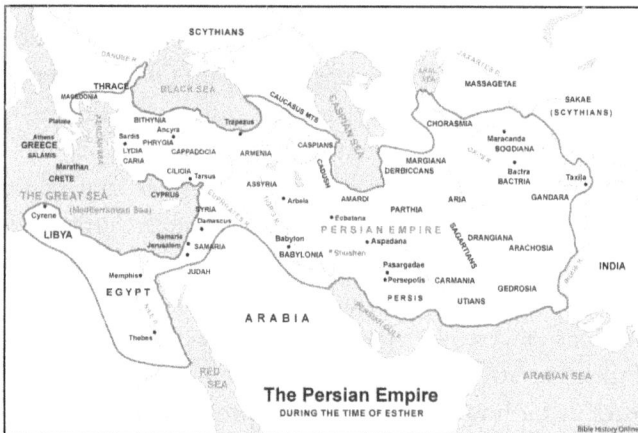

The Persian Empire
DURING THE TIME OF ESTHER

Figure 1: The Extent of the Persian Empire[1]

The first hearers of the Esther narrative were from an oral culture, like much of the world today, including many in Asia. In oral cultures, narrative

---

1. *Shushan* is also known as "Susa." See http://www.bible-history.com/maps/images/esther_persian_empire.jpg.

is the key to passing on traditions such as history, identity, religion, and how to live. It is difficult to date the book of Esther because it could have first circulated in oral form, and then sources might have been added before it was compiled into the final version. The original audience for the book roughly corresponds to when it was written, which is probably during the Persian Period. The language used is late biblical Hebrew,[2] and there is a lack of Greek words. The narrative reveals an intimate knowledge of Persian customs and its court and postal system. Like many OT books, Esther does not mention who wrote it, although it is written sometime after the events of the book. Esther 9 mentions that Purim was already being celebrated, and the book was written to regulate its observance. The mention of the recording of the events of Xerxes' reign in annals also suggests some time has passed (10:2). Although most scholars date the book of Esther to the Greek Period (fourth or third century BC), a late fifth to early fourth century BC date seems more likely, with the original audience primarily Jews in Persia.[3]

The version of Esther on which this commentary is based is the Hebrew text (MT)[4] found in Protestant and Jewish Bibles, although there are two other Greek versions of Esther. People are not sure how the three texts are related, but it seems likely that one Greek version, the Septuagint (LXX), is basically a translation of the Hebrew version (MT) with added passages, known as Additions A–F. The LXX is more religious, with explicit references to God and a more pious presentation of Esther and Mordecai. The LXX is used in Roman Catholic and Orthodox churches. The Alpha Text (AT) is the second Greek version, which most scholars view as a translation of a different Hebrew text. Like the LXX, the AT mentions God, but it is about 20 percent shorter than the two other versions, mainly because it does not end with regulations for Purim. Since the MT was accepted as canonical for the Protestant church, in this commentary we will only refer to the LXX and AT for comparison and contrast.

The book of Esther is presented as history in narrative form – it is an historical narrative. The account begins with a reference to King Xerxes, who existed in time (1:1, 2, 3) and who ruled over a specific empire (1:1–2). It also includes the dates of events (1:3; 2:16; 3:7). It provides specific dates for the yearly commemoration of an event known as Purim. If this event did

---

2. Late biblical Hebrew is found in Esther, Daniel, Ezra, Nehemiah, and Chronicles.
3. The range for the date of writing is from the time of the events in the book (reign of Xerxes) to AD 94, the date of Josephus' *Antiquities*, in which he retells the narrative of Esther.
4. Masoretic Text.

not take place in reality, it becomes the "celebration of a legendary victory."[5] The account ends with a reference to Mordecai, whose high honor is "written in the book of the annals of the kings of Media and Persia" (10:2; compare 1 Kgs 14:29). Mordecai is meant to be viewed as an historical figure, whose existence can be confirmed in an external historical source, although we do not have access to this source today. The book of Esther itself tells us that we are to read it as if it is based on *historical* events and persons. This historicity is important for us in Asia who are in contact with religious systems that believe in the unreality of the world and history, such as Hinduism and Buddhism.

In this commentary, historical accounts close to the time of the narrative will be used to provide some historical background. Greek historians such as Herodotus and the Jewish historian, Josephus, will be quoted or referenced.[6] Not all events and people in the Esther account, however, can be supported by historical sources. For instance, Herodotus writes that Xerxes' wife was Amestris (7.114), not Vashti or Esther. And although Persian kings were known to take concubines for their harems from any ethnic group, they apparently only took wives from one of seven noble families (3.70–71, 84). Plausible explanations can be given,[7] but even if there is no record of this particular situation, this does not mean these events and people did not happen or exist. They might not have been recorded in the first place, the sources might be lost, or they may have not been discovered yet. Moreover, we need to keep in mind that the way they wrote history then is different from the way we write history today, so we cannot judge the historicity of events and people based on our contemporary criteria.

Indeed, the book of Esther is history in *narrative* form. As such, all narratives contain similar elements including a plot, characters, and settings.[8] Narratives are found in all cultures, and they are an effective way of presenting

5. Leslie C. Allen and Timothy S. Laniak, *Ezra, Nehemiah, Esther* (Peabody, MA: Hendrickson, 2003), 178.
6. These sources can be accessed online at http://www.perseus.tufts.edu. Every historian, however, is fallible, and bias is built into any account. For an in-depth discussion of history, history-writing, and the Bible, see Iain W. Provan, V. Philips Long, and Tremper Longman, *A Biblical History of Israel*, 2nd ed. (Louisville, KY: Westminster John Knox, 2015), 3–154.
7. Vashti could be the transliteration of the Greek name Amestris or her Persian name into Hebrew. Or it might be that Herodotus only names the wives who bore royal successors; Karen H. Jobes, *Esther*, NIVAC (Grand Rapids, MI: Zondervan, 1999), 66–67. If Esther is not the same person as Amestris, her not coming from one of the seven noble families is not more of a problem than Xerxes' mother, Atossa (Herodotus 3.88), who was also not from one of the seven families.
8. See especially Robert Alter, *The Art of Biblical Narrative* (New York: Basic Books, 1981); Adele Berlin, *Poetics and Interpretation of Biblical Narrative* (Sheffield, UK: Almond Press, 1983).

biblical truth. The audience can enter the world of the narrative, identify with the characters, feel their tension, and find relief when things are resolved by the end. A particular characteristic of the Esther narrative is its use of irony and humor. We might not be used to thinking that biblical narratives contain these elements. But they are an effective way for us to understand the viewpoint presented by the narrative. Things are not always as they seem, and life is full of surprises – these are truisms brought out by irony and humor. In the Esther narrative, irony points out the true power behind the throne; humor makes us laugh at the downfall of the enemy.[9] Narratives are thus an important way for communities to pass on ideas and ways of living to the next generation. In biblical narratives we learn about God and how he wants us to live in his world, even as he informs us and shapes us through narratives. The Esther narrative was set in ancient West Asia, yet it still has the power to move us to renewed thought and action in our Asian settings today.

As we zoom in on the details of the book of Esther in this commentary, it is helpful for us to zoom out to see its overall shape. The structure of Esther can be viewed as a reversal:[10]

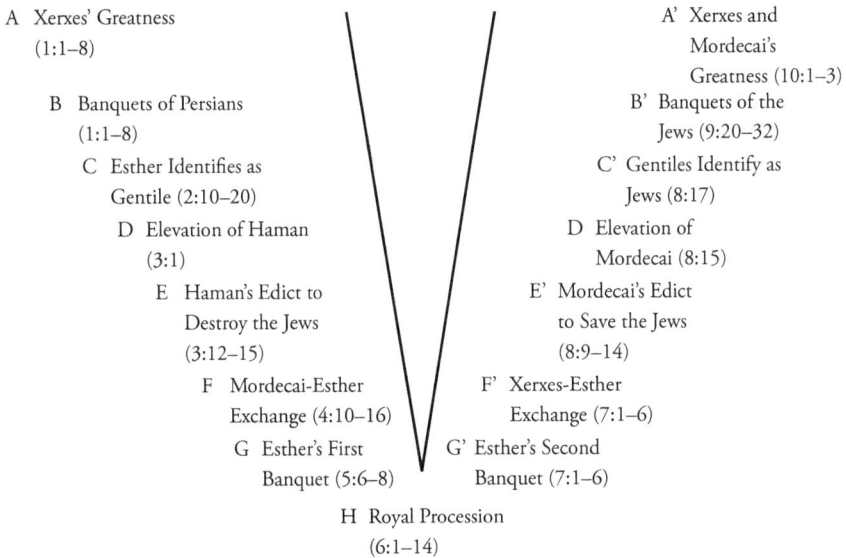

A Xerxes' Greatness (1:1–8)

  B Banquets of Persians (1:1–8)

    C Esther Identifies as Gentile (2:10–20)

      D Elevation of Haman (3:1)

        E Haman's Edict to Destroy the Jews (3:12–15)

          F Mordecai-Esther Exchange (4:10–16)

            G Esther's First Banquet (5:6–8)

A' Xerxes and Mordecai's Greatness (10:1–3)

  B' Banquets of the Jews (9:20–32)

    C' Gentiles Identify as Jews (8:17)

      D' Elevation of Mordecai (8:15)

        E' Mordecai's Edict to Save the Jews (8:9–14)

          F' Xerxes-Esther Exchange (7:1–6)

            G' Esther's Second Banquet (7:1–6)

              H Royal Procession (6:1–14)

---

9. See "The Hidden King" and "Irony" on pages 20 and 78. See also Barry G. Webb, *Five Festal Garments: Christian Reflections on the Song of Songs, Ruth, Lamentations, Ecclesiastes, Esther*, NSBT (Leicester, UK: Apollos, 2000), 131–133.
10. Slightly adapted from Jon D. Levenson, *Esther*, OTL (Louisville, KY: Westminster John Knox, 1997), 8.

This symmetrical structure shows that all the major events in the first half of the book have a parallel in the second half. To these could be added minor parallel events, such as Xerxes handing over the signet ring first to Haman (3:10) then to Mordecai (8:2).[11]

READING ESTHER IN THE CANON

Along with the original historical context, in this commentary we will read Esther in the context of the canon of Scripture. The Bible consists of many books written by various authors in different places over thousands of years. Yet despite this diversity, it has one overall divine author – God (2 Tim 3:16–17). That is why, even though the Bible has two main parts, we can read it as one big story. We read the Old Testament in light of other books in the Old Testament, and we read books in the Old Testament in light of the New Testament. It is all one story, reaching its climax in the person and work of Jesus Christ.[12]

The book of Esther itself compels us to read it within the context of other OT books. For instance, the ways Mordecai and Haman are introduced push us to consider the animosity between their peoples earlier in the Old Testament narrative. The actions and words of Esther and Haman remind us of the wise person and the fool respectively, so we recall Wisdom Literature, especially Proverbs and Ecclesiastes. The actions of Esther, Mordecai, and the Jews in the diaspora, especially their lack of specific interaction with the Lord, have us thinking about other narratives set outside the Promised Land, such as the stories of Moses and of Joseph and Daniel and his friends. An enriching dialog takes place as we read the book of Esther alongside these OT texts.

One reason we read the book of Esther in light of the New Testament is to find out how the story turns out. Like any good narrative, themes, tensions, and unfinished plotlines from the first part are developed and find completion in the second part. Jesus said that the Old Testament testifies about, points forward to, and is fulfilled in him (Luke 24:25–27, 44–45; John 5:39–40). Now that Jesus has come, there will be points of continuity and points of discontinuity for those of us who are Christians today as we move from the OT to the NT. For instance, the Jews in the book of Esther were under the old covenant, but they looked forward to a new covenant, as most clearly

---

11. See "Reversals" on page 112.
12. See Craig G. Bartholomew and Michael W. Goheen, *The Drama of Scripture: Finding Our Place in the Biblical Story* (Grand Rapids, MI: Baker Academic, 2004); Vaughan Roberts, *God's Big Picture: Tracing the Storyline of the Bible* (Leicester, UK: IVP Books, 2003).

anticipated by Jeremiah (Jer 31:31–34). Jesus inaugurates and mediates the new covenant, so we are now under the new covenant (Luke 22:19–20; Heb 8:6–13). The people of God are now those who are "in Christ" – Christians.[13] As the Apostle Paul says, "In Christ Jesus you are all children of God through faith. There is neither Jew nor Gentile, neither slave nor free, nor is there male and female, for you are all one in Christ Jesus . . . . If you belong to Christ, then you are Abraham's seed, and heirs according to the promise" (Gal 3:26, 28–29). All people who belong to Christ are God's people, part of God's family, whether ethnically Jewish or not.

Furthermore, people, events, and institutions in the OT anticipate, and can find greater meaning in, the NT especially in the life and work of Jesus. These are called "types," which look forward to their fulfilment in Jesus. In the Esther narrative God delivered his people from destruction, just like he did in the Exodus. One way this connection is hinted at in the narrative is through the date of the issue of Haman's planned annihilation, the thirteenth day of the first month (Esth 3:12), which is the day before Passover (Exod 12:6). As we look back to God's deliverance of his people from bondage in Egypt, we also look forward to God's greatest deliverance of his people from bondage to Satan, sin, and death in Jesus. In this commentary people will be viewed as types, such as Esther and Mordecai. Like other people in the OT they are imperfect, yet God still uses them to bring "rest" and "peace" for his people. This looks forward to a greater "rest" and "peace" that the perfect Jesus will win for us.

Reading the Esther narrative in the context of the canon of Scripture also helps us work out theology and ethics. It can be difficult to work out what an OT narrative is telling us about God and how we should live. Especially so in a narrative that does not mention God, and the people of God did not do anything religious or even speak of him. Comparing the Esther narrative with other OT narratives, especially those in which God is silent or absent, can help us work out what this narrative says about God and how he works. Examining what the characters did and did not do in light of God's clear teaching in other parts of the OT, such as the law, helps us to evaluate them. After we work out some ethical principles from the Esther narrative, we can also look at them through the lens of Christ and the NT. This is when points of continuity and discontinuity will come into focus, which we will need to take into account before we apply the principles to ourselves today. For example, what did Jesus

---

13. See also "Land, Covenant, Temple, King, People" on page 100.

teach about how we should treat our enemies? What did the Apostle Paul teach about how a husband should treat his wife? Instead of Purim, how can Christians commemorate their deliverance by God?

READING ESTHER IN ASIA

All narratives, including historical narratives such as Esther, contain themes and motifs. Themes are major ideas that recur in a narrative, while motifs are minor elements that recur and can contribute to a theme. An Asian setting sensitizes us to particular themes and motifs in the Esther narrative.

As noted above, "reversal" is a major theme that is reflected in the structure of the book of Esther. Many smaller reversals contribute to the overall reversal in the narrative, and behind these is the hidden hand of God, who influenced the narrative like an off-stage director. Although God is not named, there are too many "coincidences" in the narrative for them to happen by "chance" or by "luck." This might be difficult to accept within a Western worldview that holds onto scientific explanations and excludes the supernatural, but it is a view which is more acceptable in most of Asia today, where consciousness of the divine or supernatural pervades all of life and where there is not such a strong "sacred/secular" divide. Superstitions seep into all areas of life in Asia, in relation to numbers and dates, locations of houses and placement of furniture, what foods to eat and what clothes to wear, and more. Similarly, Haman the Agagite believed in some greater force as he cast "lots" (*Pur*) to determine the most auspicious day for his planned annihilation of the Jews. In the OT, the outcome of the casting of lots was determined by God (Prov 16:33), so ironically, even though Haman thought he was determining the fate of God's people, in reality God was controlling the destiny of the lot and his people. Intriguingly, the Jews were not described as doing anything clearly religious, and they did not mention God in their speech. Yet themes can even be discerned in this seeming absence of God.

God's "absence" is in reality his hiddenness; he influences all of life even when we do not see him or his actions. One effect of God's hiddenness in the Esther narrative is to highlight the courage and initiative of the Jewish main characters. They might not be perfect role models, but at least in this respect they can be followed. Mordecai took a stand against Haman, which began the conflict with the Jews, Haman, and the rest of the Jews' enemies. Esther resolved to approach King Xerxes, even at the risk of losing her life. A large part of these actions is based upon values that many Asians understand intuitively. Mordecai acted on the basis of the largest social group that he belonged to – the Jewish people (Esth 3:3–4). Esther was persuaded to act on the basis of the smallest social group that she belonged to – her father's house (4:14). Asian societies in which collectives are a more central component of identity can thus understand the importance of loyalty to ethnic group and family. At times, we as Christians will also need to courageously identify with Christ in threatening situations. That God was hidden in the Esther narrative leaves a gap for the audience to fill in as they read the narrative: the Jews fasted and prayed to God; relief and deliverance came from God. Paradoxically, our perception of God's influence is heightened, and our loyalty to him is aroused by his absence.[14]

Feasting is a motif that is also closely connected to the reversal theme. Feasting plays an important role in Asian cultures and is a prominent part of the structure of Esther. Michael Fox notes that the feasts in the book of Esther are "the sites of important events and . . . signal shifts of power."[15] In our structure, they are found at important points, at the beginning and end, and surrounding the turning point of the Esther narrative. The opening two feasts established the power and grandeur of the Persian Empire under King Xerxes. At the feasts of Esther in the center of the narrative, she made her request to the king, and Haman's fate was sealed. The Jews feasted for two days at the end of the book, as they celebrated their deliverance. The importance of the feasting motif in the structure is consistent with a book that explains the establishment of an ongoing Jewish feast – Purim. Like the Passover Feast, the theme underlying Purim is the deliverance of God. The first deliverance was through the miraculous and the supernatural. The second was through the divine influence over the natural. Just as God acted in the first deliverance because of the covenant he made with Israel's forefathers – Abraham, Isaac and Jacob (Exod 2:23–25) – so in Purim we are reminded that God acted on the basis of the same covenant. Although many of God's people in the Esther narrative did not seem conscious of him in their day-to-day lives and even though Esther contravened his dietary and intermarriage laws, God remained steadfastly faithful to his covenant people. Moreover, they can still be his covenant people even though they are outside the Promised Land, without access to the Temple.[16]

---

14. See "Identify Yourself" on page 56.
15. Michael V. Fox, *Character and Ideology in the Book of Esther*, 2nd ed. (Grand Rapids, MI: Eerdmans, 2001), 156.
16. See "Land, Covenant, Temple, King, People" on page 100.

The theme of faithful living in the diaspora has relevance both for the original audience in the time of the Persian Empire and for Christians in Asia today. They are outside the Promised Land. We find some "rest" in Christ (Matt 28:18–20), but we are still exiles looking forward to our final rest and promised inheritance (Heb 4:1–11; 1 Pet 1:1–5). They lived under a foreign authority whose tolerance could swing to hostility at the whim of such a malevolent leader. We live under governments that are either non-Christian or outright anti-Christian. In Asia, as in other parts of the world, we have seen how long-serving leaders in democracies can over time act more like dictators, silencing or oppressing Christian minorities. The Esther narrative shows us one way that we as Christians can live under such governments. We can work with and within our political-social structures, remaining loyal to the government and promoting the prosperity of our countries (Jer 29:7). Yet this does not mean that we need to agree with all its decisions. We can be agents of transformation for the good of our society. And since the Esther narrative reveals that God's hidden hand is always working, Christian politicians and leaders can act responsibly and wisely and then trust the outcome of their decisions to God.[17]

---

17. See "Esther and Politics" on page 67.

ESTHER 1

Most of us in Malaysia do not feel comfortable criticizing our leaders in public. We prefer to show respect in public so that they can maintain "face." Unlike those living in some Western countries, such as Australia, we do not even feel comfortable addressing our elders and superiors without using a title, such as "Aunty," "Pastor," or "Doctor." Certainly, many of us in Malaysia do not like to give negative feedback to our leaders to their faces, even if they seek it first.

Yet, at times, we still feel the urge to voice our disapproval of a leader. We mostly do this subtly, often just to friends or colleagues, behind the back of the leader. Depending on our relationship to the leader, it might be possible and even preferable to voice our critique directly to the leader with gentleness and in a constructive manner. In modern democratic societies, people who are unhappy with the government can express their discontent through various channels, such as writing letters to the local parliamentary member, signing petitions, and ultimately by voting for certain political parties. For Jews living under the Persian Empire, however, these means of voicing disapproval were not available.

As the narrative of Esther begins, we are introduced to the king of the Persian Empire. In Esther 1 we find a subtle critique of King Xerxes. It is not directly spoken, but if we look closely at how the narrative presents the king and his actions, we will see that the critique is there, nonetheless. Indeed, in the narrative we can detect a mocking tone towards the king.

As we look at this chapter, we will find that the critique is not driven by disillusionment, bitterness, or a desire to bring down the empire. It is driven by the desire of the author of Esther to reveal to us the reality of who is truly sitting on the throne of the universe.

We will examine this chapter in three scenes. The first scene focuses on the power and the wealth of the Persian king and his excesses (vv. 1–8). In the second scene, we see the power of the king starting to be undermined, when his wife, the queen, refused to obey his command (vv. 9–12). The final scene reveals how the king and his advisors responded to the rebellious action of the queen (vv. 13–22).

1:1–8 SCENE 1: THE KING FEASTED

The first thing we notice about King Xerxes is that he was powerful.[1] He was the king of a vast empire of 127 provinces (v. 1).[2] On today's map, this empire would stretch from India to Sudan, and include countries such as NW India, Pakistan, Armenia, Iran, Iraq, Lebanon, Jordan, Syria, Israel, N Greece, N Turkey, Egypt, Libya, Ethiopia, and N Sudan, among others. It was the world empire of the day. Indeed, for those living in the Persian Empire, it was their whole known world.[3]

King Xerxes was not only powerful, he was also rich. And he liked to display his wealth. So, in the third year of his reign, he gave a "feast" (*mishteh*) for the most important people in his kingdom – all his nobles, officials, military leaders, and princes (v. 3).[4] *Mishteh* has a strong association with drinking, a fact that will become important later in this chapter.[5] This feast lasted for 180 days – half a year! With the rich variety of food available in Malaysia, one of the cherished pastimes is to *makan* (eat). This is especially so on holidays, when it would not be unusual for a Malaysian to eat up to six times a day. Malaysians would gladly accept King Xerxes as an honorary citizen.

After the king's six-month feast, he held another feast, this time in the courtyard of his palace garden. It was for "all the people from the least to the greatest," so we think it is for both men and women. When we read later that Queen Vashti had a separate feast for the women only (v. 9), we realize that this second banquet was for men only. King Xerxes' second banquet took place in the citadel, or fortress, of Susa. The Persian Empire had four capital cities: Pasargadae, Babylon, Ecbatana, and Susa. Susa was the administrative center and the king's winter residence. From here, "he displayed the vast wealth of his kingdom and the splendor and glory of his majesty" (v. 4). In this description, we find an avalanche of grandiose words. The point is that the king was wealthy, and he wanted to show it off. How rich was the king? If you read the

---

1. King Xerxes is also known as King Ahasuerus (e.g., ESV, NRSV, NKJV, NJPS). He took over the Persian Empire at its territorial peak from his father, King Darius I. King Xerxes is known for his invasion of Greece, with his defeat marking the beginning of the decline of the Persian Empire. For a brief overview of his life and reign, see Jean-Louis Huot. "Xerxes I" in *Encyclopædia Britannica*, available online at https://www.britannica.com/biography/Xerxes-I (accessed November 30, 2017). For further information on the Achaemenid Empire, see R. Schmitt, "Achaemenid Dynasty," *Encyclopædia Iranica*, available online at http://www.iranicaonline.org/articles/achaemenid-dynasty (accessed November 30, 2017).
2. Compare with Daniel 6:1, where King Darius rules over 120 satraps.
3. Frederic W. Bush, *Ruth, Esther*, WBC 9 (Dallas, TX: Word Books, 1996), 353.
4. Since King Xerxes reigned from 486–465 BC, his third year was 483 BC.
5. BDB, 1059.

description of the palace in verse 6, it is a riot of luxurious materials, furniture, and precious stones. No doubt, many of these items would have been either plunder from or tributes paid by conquered territories (2:18; 10:1).

Some rich people in Malaysia like to hide their wealth. They walk around in threadbare clothes and drive around in 20-year-old Toyotas. Other rich people like to show off their wealth by wearing Armani suits and driving around in the latest-model Mercedes. We know which category King Xerxes would fall into. The couches in his palace were made from the precious metals we use for making jewelry. The pavement you step on had precious stones that we normally wear around our necks! The king's palace would rival the new Istana Negara (National Palace) in Kuala Lumpur, Malaysia![6]

At this luscious banquet in the king's opulent palace, free-flow wine was on offer from the king's wine stewards. Literally, "the drinking was according to *dat* (law/edict); there was no one compelling" (v. 8.). The king was generous, although in the Persian Empire, even drinking without restraint required an official order from the king. The wine was served in golden goblets (compare with Dan 5:3), each of them different (vv. 7–8). And the wine was served by wine stewards who were on hand to top up your wine goblet as soon as it emptied. It all sets your head spinning as you try to put the images of the palace together on top of the dizzying effect of too much wine.

But that's the point: in this description, the narrator wants us to experience and begin to taste this extravagant, excessive, over-the-top banquet. You think wedding banquets in Malaysia are grand? They are like an afternoon tea compared to King Xerxes' banquets.

Why did King Xerxes hold these banquets at this point of time in his reign? At this time, the king was probably preparing to launch an invasion of Greece.[7] So these feasts were his way of gaining support for his upcoming attack. You know how the saying goes, "There is no such thing as a free . . . feast." If the king gave a generous feast, the expectation was that his officials and leaders and subjects would give something in return. In this case, the king wanted their loyalty.

Let us put ourselves in the sandals of those who attended the king's banquets. We come as common people, and the king treats us like royalty. How might we respond? On the one hand, we might not be as powerful or rich,

6. Opened in 2011, it is estimated that it cost RM812 million (approx. USD 190 million) to build; available online at https://en.wikipedia.org/wiki/Istana_Negara,_Jalan_Duta, November 15, 2016.
7. See Karen H. Jobes, *Esther,* NIVAC (Grand Rapids, MI: Zondervan, 1999), 60–61.

but we might grow envious of those who are wealthy like King Xerxes. After getting a taste of his lifestyle and knowing the influence he has, would it not be natural to feel a little envious? But as Christians, remember what the Apostle Paul says: "godliness with contentment is great gain" and "the love of money is the root of all kinds of evil" (1 Tim 6:6–10).

On the other hand, some of us are not tempted by the king's riches and power because God has already blessed us with these. But have we felt the temptation to trust in our wealth and so have become arrogant? The Apostle Paul has advice for us also: continue to trust in God, be rich in good deeds, and be generous (1 Tim 6:17–19).

So, this is our introduction to King Xerxes. He has immense riches and power, beyond compare and almost beyond belief. How will he use them in the narrative of Esther?

1:9–12 SCENE 2: THE QUEEN REFUSED

Like the king, Queen Vashti also threw a banquet – for the women in the royal palace (v. 9). The fact is just stated without any description or embellishment, so we as readers are struck by its contrast with King Xerxes' extravagance. Esther provided a banquet for King Xerxes and Haman later in the narrative, so it was not the case that men and women were always separated for feasts in Persian custom. We do not know why they were separated for these banquets. What we do know is that Vashti's banquet took place in "the royal palace of King Xerxes." We are reminded again of the dominance of the king, even though he was absent from the women's banquet.

By the seventh day of the king's second feast, King Xerxes "was in high spirits from wine" (v. 10). According to the Bible, it is not wrong to drink wine, and at times it is even commended (e.g., Eccl 9:7). The problem comes when we drink too much wine, for it can lead an inebriated person astray and make a mockery of them (Prov 20:1). In the OT, we have Noah and Lot as such examples (Gen 9:20–26; 19:30–38). After a week-long banquet involving unlimited wine, King Xerxes' "heart" (*leb*) was "merry (*tob*; literally, "good") with wine" (v. 10; ESV). This phrase can mean "glad of heart" (e.g., 1 Kgs 8:66) or under the influence of alcohol (e.g., 1 Sam 25:36). After drinking wine for a week, the king was probably, at the very least, tipsy and most likely to be outright drunk. In Hebrew thinking, the "heart" (*leb*) is the seat of the emotions and intellect.[8] Now that the king's judgment was impaired, we expect that something bad is about to happen. Perhaps even something for which he could end up being mocked.

And something does happen. The king thought it was a good idea to parade his wife, the queen, in front of a crowd of drunken men. He showed off his objects of power and wealth, and now he wanted to show off another object – his wife. Note that verse 11 does not say that he wanted her to come to join him in his celebrations. The verse also does not say that he wanted her to come to meet his colleagues and friends. Instead, it says to bring her before him, "in order to display her beauty to the people and the nobles, for she was lovely to look at." In this verse, we are told twice about her stunning beauty. In today's language, King Xerxes wanted to show off his shiny trophy wife.

So, typical of his extravagance, he commanded not one, but seven of his eunuchs to summon the queen from her own banquet. In ancient West Asia, a eunuch was a male servant or official in the court of a ruler. He was often castrated, and commonly oversaw the harem of the king.[9] We see eunuchs fulfilled these roles in the book of Esther. In verse 10, king Xerxes sent them to fetch his queen. Perhaps he knew the resistance he would meet, so that he needed a show of strength to try and convince her to do what he is about to request. The large number of eunuchs attending the king, along with the king's seven advisors (v. 14) certainly added to the grandeur of the royal court.[10] Readers in Malaysia can appreciate the exalted status of the king but also detect a sense of redundancy and inefficiency within the Persian government.

In any case, in response to the king, Queen Vashti said, "No" (v. 12).[11] Today, in modern monarchies, we can imagine that a queen can refuse a king, or at least discuss a matter with him. But in the context of ancient West Asia, the queen should have "known her place" and obeyed her superior; unless she had strong reasons not to. The narrative, however, does not provide a reason

---

8. BDB, 525.

9. For more background about eunuchs in Persia, see Muhammad Dandamayev, "Eunuchs, Archemenid Period," in *Encyclopædia Iranica*, available online at http://www.iranicaonline.org/articles/eunuchs (accessed December 1, 2017). Eunuchs are found in the OT, including employees of Israelite kings (e.g., 2 Kgs 9:32). According to the Law, they were to be excluded from the assembly of God's people (Deut 23:1), although their exclusion changes towards the end of the OT (Isa 56:3–5). Eunuchs are still present in the time of Jesus (Matt 19:12) and the early church, when an Ethiopian eunuch is baptized (Acts 8:26–39).

10. Bush, *Ruth, Esther*, 349: the naming of the seven eunuchs adds "to the solemnity and pomposity of the occasion."

11. Vashti does not speak in the narrative; her response is simply reported in the third person (v. 12).

for Vashti's refusal. Verse 11 says that she was asked to come to the king's banquet "wearing her royal crown," but it does not mention anything else. Some Jewish midrashic accounts suggest that the king commanded her to appear only wearing a crown and nothing else.[12] This seems unlikely, although it does bring out the inappropriate nature of the king's request. Plutarch (AD 46–120) wrote that the wives of Persian kings sat beside them at dinner but left when the kings wished to get drunk. At this point, they sent for "their dancing girls and concubines."[13] If this is the case, we can understand why Vashti refused – she was about to be dishonored as a concubine.

Anyway, we are left in no doubt about the king's response. His authority was threatened before the people. He was dishonored; he lost "face" before his subjects. From the king's perspective, even though his request was not the norm, the queen still should have obeyed. We can understand why the king's response was so strong, even excessive: he was "furious," and he "burned with anger" (v. 12). The honor of this generous monarch had been building and building up to this point, but now it all exploded in his face. We can picture his face turned beetroot red and the smoke coming out of his ears. This would not be the last time that we see a character enraged in the Esther narrative.

What do we have here? Irony. The most powerful man in the world, who ruled over 127 provinces, did not have power over one woman in his own household. The queen did not obey the almighty king.

1:13–22 SCENE 3: THE KING RESPONDED

We gain more insight into the character of King Xerxes in the last scene of this chapter. We wonder if the king is able to make decisions by himself. Certainly, the disagreement between the king and his wife was played out in public. And it is commendable that the king did not act rashly. He sought the counsel of his advisors before he acted. But what was essentially a domestic issue was turned into a state affair. At its core, this was a personal problem between a husband and a wife, so it would seem more prudent to have dealt with it in private. We will keep observing the king to see how he treated problems later in the narrative.

---

12. For references to the midrashic material, along with a discussion of these, see Tamar Kadari, "Vashti: Midrash and Aggadah," in *Jewish Women: A Comprehensive Historical Encyclopedia*, Jewish Women's Archive, available online at https://jwa.org/encyclopedia/article/vashti-midrash-and-aggadah (accessed December 1, 2017).
13. Plutarch, *Morals* 4.16. See http://www.gutenberg.org/files/23639/23639-h/23639-h.htm#Page_70.

Now that the king had lost "face," he turned to his "wise men who knew the times," experts in the Persian law, to find out what to do (v. 13). These seven princes of Persia and Media were his closest advisors, who were able to see "the king's face," and who "sat first in the kingdom" (v. 14; esv). That is, they had the privilege of speaking to him directly, face-to-face. The king asked them, "Under the law (dt)," how do we deal with a disobedient queen? (v. 15). Again, the Persian law was brought into play (1:8). However, there was probably no provision under the law for this because Memucan, the spokesman of the king's advisors, did not answer the king's question directly.

Instead, he sidetracked by forecasting the effect of the queen's offence. He first asserted that Queen Vashti's crime was not just against the king, but also against all people in the kingdom (v. 16). He then speculated that the queen's disobedience would trigger widespread mini-rebellions: wives would now despise and disrespect their husbands throughout the Persian Empire (v. 17). As if to underline his point, the narrator used ba'al ("lord") instead of 'iysh ("man") to refer to husbands. This contempt will begin immediately in the households of the king's nobles and will lead to "no end" (Heb. day; "more than enough") of contempt and anger (v. 18)!

Perhaps Memucan had detected an undercurrent of domestic defiance in some or all parts of the Persian Empire, and he now saw this as an opportunity to suppress it. But even today, any form of insubordination by a wife is still frowned upon in Malaysia and many parts of Asia. It thus seems unlikely that this would have been taking place in the West Asian cultural context of Persia. So, like his monarch, Memucan was probably overreacting and thus overstated his case.

To counter this perceived threat to authority, Memucan then suggested drafting a new Persian law that banned Queen Vashti from entering the presence of the king (v. 19). Memucan introduced his suggestion by using the phrase, "If it pleases the king." Literally, "if upon the king it is good"; that is, "upon the king" is placed at the front of the phrase, emphasizing Memucan's deference to him.[14] This attitude towards the king was in contrast to that displayed by the Queen. And the exact phrase, unique to the book of Esther, is used again at points of tension in the Esther narrative (3:9; 5:4, 8; 7:3; 8:5; 9:13). An aspect of Persian law mentioned by Memucan sets up another important factor for the plot of the Esther narrative: Persian law cannot be repealed (similar to Dan 6:8, 12, 15). Even the king was not at liberty to act against it.

---

14. John Screnock and Robert D. Holmstedt, *Esther: A Handbook on the Hebrew Text* (Waco, TX: Baylor University Press, 2015), 66.

So, ironically, what Queen Vashti refused to do would now become a written decree. She was to be removed as queen and her position given to another. For the first time in the chapter, she was referred to as only "Vashti," as if she had already been demoted to the king's harem.[15] Her replacement would be one who was "better than she."[16] Better in what respect? In the immediate context, we would presume her successor would be more submissive, for Vashti had been removed because of her insubordination. Time will tell, however, if her successor could survive under the Persian law. Perhaps also "better" in the sense that she would be a better example to the rest of the women in the Persian Empire.[17] For when the king's edict to ban Vashti from his presence was proclaimed throughout his empire, it would frighten all women into respecting their husbands (v. 20)!

The king and his nobles liked Memucan's advice and so followed the general outline of his proposal (v. 21). Yet the king also added a twist to the proclamation. The letters he dispatched to every corner of his kingdom added that "every man should be ruler (sarar) over his own household, using his native tongue" (v. 22). The word for "ruler" (sarar) in this verse has the same root as that for a palace "official," "noble" or "prince" (sar) used in 1:3, 11, 14, 16, 18, and 21. In other words, every ordinary man could now be like one of the nobles or officials in the palace. Any husband who read this decree must have been smirking to himself. I'm picturing each husband strutting around like little kings of their own little castles.

And each man's authority was reinforced by the use of his "native tongue" (v. 22). Within the Persian Empire, there would have been mixed-marriage households where more than one language was spoken. This was also the case in the time of Ezra and Nehemiah (Neh 13:23–24). King Xerxes' proclamation allowed the husband to enforce the use of his language at home.

And so, the king's decree was dispatched by royal mail to every far-flung corner of his kingdom (v. 22). The Greek historian Herodotus claimed that the Persians invented this courier system. It is said that there were as many horses and men posted at intervals as there were days required for the entire journey, so that one horse and one man were assigned to each day. The first

---

15. She is referred to as "Queen Vashti" five times before this verse (1:9, 11, 12, 15, 16), then only "Vashti" in this verse and in the next chapter (2:1, 4, 17).

16. Compare with 1 Samuel 15:28, where Saul is told he will be replaced.

17. See David Clarence, "Esther," in *South Asia Bible Commentary: A One-Volume Commentary on the Whole Bible*, ed. Brian C. Wintle (Grand Rapids, MI: Zondervan, 2015), 569. As the narrative progresses, we will find that she is "better" in another sense also (2:7).

courier passed on the instructions to the second, the second to the third, and from there they were transmitted from one to another all the way through.[18] One estimate is that it would take three months for a message to spread throughout the Persian Empire.[19] The efficient Persian administration ensured that all people groups would understand the king's proclamation, since it was written in the specific language of the people of each province.

Throughout Asia, language is a core component of ethnic identity. This is no different in Malaysia. Since 1967 *Bahasa Malaysia* has been the official and national language, as well as the medium of instruction in most national schools and most universities. As we look at the Persian decree in this chapter, we marvel at the tolerance of the Persian Empire towards different ethnic groups under its dominion. Each ethnic group was allowed to maintain its own language, and hence a core component of its identity.

Yet the outcome of this decree is ironic. Most people in the kingdom probably would not have heard of the king's "loss of face." But they certainly would now, and upon hearing it in their own language, they would fully understand!

As we reflect further on the king's decree, we realize how ridiculous it is. For you cannot legislate for a person to respect another. You cannot demand that someone respect you. Within a marriage, respect is to be encouraged, but we know from the Apostle Paul that this is only half of the equation. Yes, wives should respect their husbands; but husbands also need to love their wives, "just as Christ loved the church and gave himself up for her" (Eph 5:25, 33). Indeed, the Apostle Peter says that husbands should be "considerate" and treat their wives "with respect" (1 Pet 3:7). I wonder if King Xerxes loved and respected his wife Vashti like this?

In much of Asia the patriarch still dominates, although in different local forms.[20] At times this form of society in which the men hold primary power in the political, moral, and social spheres leads to their abuse of power. Yet the Bible, including the NT quotations above, is written within this context. Both men and women are created in the image of God and are thus equal before him (Gen 1:26–27). Although we have different roles, we are to treat each other with respect as God's image bearers.

---

18. Herodotus 8.98.
19. Herodotus 5.50–54.
20. For a comparison of patriarchs in South and North Korea, China, Taiwan, and Japan, see Kaku Sechiyama, *Patriarchy in East Asia: A Comparative Sociology of Gender,* trans. James Smith (Leiden, Netherlands: Brill, 2013).

THE HIDDEN KING

In the NIV, the word "king" or "kingdom" occurs 29 times in this chapter. We cannot mistake that Xerxes was the king of a vast, powerful, and wealthy kingdom. Most scholars do not think the Persian kings considered themselves to be gods. There was some evidence, however, that the kings were considered divine, as shown in this quote from the pseudo-Aristotelian *de mundo*:

> For the court of Cambyses, Xerxes and Darius were splendidly adorned for ceremonious and brilliant eminence. He himself, as it is heard, sat on the throne in Susa or Ecbatana, invisible to all, in a wonderful royal castle and palace domain sparkling with gold, electrum and ivory . . . . And outside there stood, decked and ready, the first and most distinguished men . . . so that the king himself, who was addressed as sovereign and god, might see and hear everything.[1]

Esther 1 lends some weight to this view, as King Xerxes showed off the "splendor and glory (*kevod*) of his majesty" (v. 4). The lavish description of the palace reminds us of the decorations of the tabernacle and temple (Exod 25–40; 1 Kgs 6–7). In the book of Daniel too, royalty skirted close to deity (Dan 3, 6).[2] Yet in the Bible, "glory" (*kevod*) is most closely associated with the LORD God. Whether or not the narrator used this word intentionally, we, as readers of the Bible, are wary of its association with a human king.

Asian people have had some experience with kings and empires. Much of Asia was under colonial rule for at least some time, and in recent history, most countries gained independence after the end of World War II. For instance, Malaya gained independence from British rule in 1957, and "Malaysia" was formed in 1963. Malaysia still has a monarchy, but it is more in name only. The Malaysian kings do not exert the same wide-reaching power that the kings in the Persian Empire did.

Wherever we might live in Asia, most of us cannot escape another type of powerful empire – the effects of globalization. Airplanes, mobile phones, and especially the internet has led to the spread of people, knowledge, trade, and money (among other things), across our globe. As such, we increasingly live under powerful global "empires." Some of these include the multi-national companies, the media, Hollywood, and the Korean Wave. All of them exert their influence on us. Just like a rich and powerful king and his kingdom, these new-world empires espouse values that can look and sound extravagant, attractive, and enticing. They might not use royal mail, but the internet, social media, and advertising now are much more efficient and pernicious. Transmission of messages and ideas across the globe now takes milliseconds, not months.

Yet the mocking tone of the narrative alerts us to the possibility that not all was as it seemed. The irony in the narrative helps to expose King Xerxes as he really was: indecisive, weak, foolish, hollow. The narrator wanted to reveal the reality behind the veneer of wealth and power in the world – that of the original hearers and readers, and us today.

For the OT reveals that there is another king who wants us to laugh with him at the visible, human kings and empires of this world. Psalm 2 tells us that "the kings of the earth take their stand against the Lord and his anointed."[3] So often, governments and "world empires," and global corporations like Apple and Toyota and Amazon, set themselves up against God. The media and the entertainment industry, such as Hollywood and Bollywood, set themselves up against the values of God's kingdom. Yet God in heaven scoffs at them (Ps 2:1–6). He laughs at the pretensions of the empires of the world.

Do we find ourselves being swayed by the advertising of the powerful global corporations? We need to remember what John wrote in 1 John 2:15–17:

> Do not love the world or anything in the world . . . . For everything in the world – the lust of the flesh, the lust of the eyes, and the pride of life – comes not from the Father but from the world. The world and its desires pass away, but whoever does the will of God lives forever.

The values of today's world empires may look and sound extravagant, attractive, and enticing. But when we stop to reflect, we will find their values hollow and temporary, and maybe even laughable.

For God has installed his king. One who, ironically, willingly disrobed on a cross. This king willingly became weak and endured shame for the sake of his subjects. Yet God raised him as the king of the universe (Phil 2:6–11). Surely, we can say, "No," when we are tempted to follow the values of worldly empires because we serve such a king. For we look forward to the most sumptuous and satisfying banquets when our King Jesus returns again (Rev 19:7–9).

---

1. As quoted in Josef Wiesehöfer, *Ancient Persia: From 550 BC to 650 AD,* trans. Azizeh Azodi (London, UK: I. B. Tauris, 2001), 34.
2. Leslie C. Allen and Timothy S. Laniak, *Ezra, Nehemiah, Esther* (Peabody, MA: Hendrickson, 2003), 200.
3. For a more detailed discussion of Psalm 2, see Federico G. Villanueva, *Psalms 1–72: A Commentary,* ABCS (Carlisle, UK: Langham Global Library, 2016), 29–33.

ESTHER 2:1–23

Some of us in Asia live under governments that do not always use power for the good of all. At times, those in power use their position for their own gain or even to oppress citizens or those from particular ethnic or religious groups. In this context, there are four main ways we can respond: resistance, submission, "active support,"[1] or by fleeing.

In Esther 1 we were introduced to King Xerxes, the king of a vast, wealthy empire. His empire was powerful, but behind the shiny exterior of his kingdom we find a fragile and vulnerable character. We saw how King Xerxes used the power entrusted to him when he dismissed his wife for insubordination. In chapter 2, his misuse of power, especially his mistreatment of women (although allowed by Persian custom), comes into full view.

Under these circumstances, how should the people of God act? In Esther 1 we also reflected on the presence of another king who is at work in the world – God. God's presence in the narrative was hidden by the narrator, but God can be found working behind the scenes by those with eyes to see him. Just like in the Esther narrative, his presence and action are often hidden from us in our day-to-day lives. We will see what Esther 2 reveals about God and how we should respond to him. In all of life, the people of God should live in response to who God is and what he has done.

We will also follow the actions of two members of God's people, Mordecai and Esther. In particular, we will see if they responded to the Persian Empire with resistance, submission, active support, or by fleeing. Which of these responses, if any, are consistent with how they should have lived as God's people? And what can we learn from this chapter about how we might live as God's people under a government that at times misuses its power?

In chapter 2, King Xerxes sought a new queen to replace Vashti (vv. 1–11). After a prolonged preparation, Esther had her turn with him (vv. 12–14), and she was chosen as the new queen (vv. 15–18). The chapter ends with Mordecai foiling an assassination attempt against King Xerxes (vv. 19–22).

---

1. Compare Yoram Hazony, *God and Politics in Esther,* 2nd ed. (Cambridge, UK: Cambridge University Press, 2016), 19.

2:1–11 SCENE 1: THE KING SOUGHT A NEW QUEEN

As the curtain is raised on the next scene, King Xerxes had sobered up and calmed down. He then remembered that he had banished his queen and that he needed to find a replacement (v. 1). Just as in chapter 1, he did not come up with a plan by himself. The "young men (*na'ar*) who attended the king"[2] made a suggestion to him: "Let's have a competition to find another stunning beauty who will please the king" (vv. 2–4; paraphrased). Beautiful queens and large harems were royal status symbols in ancient West Asia. The Jewish historian Josephus, who wrote around AD 93–94, numbered Xerxes' harem at four hundred.[3] What is thought to be Xerxes' harem complex at Persepolis has been excavated and restored.[4] Darius III (336–330 BC) was said to have between 329–365 concubines.[5] King Solomon had 600 royal wives and 300 concubines (1 Kgs 11:3). This advice from the young men to replace Vashti pleased the king, so he accepted it.

Then, a little unexpectedly, we are introduced to a Jew, Mordecai (v. 5). "Mordecai" is a Babylonian name and sounds like the name of the Babylonian god, Marduk. Either Mordecai, or more likely, Kish, one of his ancestors, was taken as captive when King Nebuchadnezzar first captured Jerusalem (597 BC; see 2 Kgs 24:10–17).[6] Since Kish was deported along with King Jehoiachin (v. 6), it is likely that Mordecai's family was among the ruling class of Judah. In any case, with the introduction of Mordecai we might be thinking, "What does he have to do with anything?" Yet as we read on, it is revealed that he had a cousin whom he brought up as his own daughter when she was orphaned. The king sought young, unmarried, beautiful women. Esther fit the bill and more: she also had a "lovely figure" (v. 7).

Just like Mordecai, Esther's name sounds like that of a Babylonian god, Ishtar. Her name also sounds like the Persian word for "star." Yet unlike Mordecai, we are also told that she had a Hebrew name, Hadassah (which

---

2. Literally, "the young men of the king, who attended him." This phrase is translated as "the king's personal attendants" (NIV) and "the king's young men who attended him" (ESV).
3. Josephus, *Antiquities of the Jews,* trans. William Whiston, 11.6.2. Available online at http://www.sacred-texts.com/jud/josephus/ant-11.htm (accessed December 4, 2017).
4. For a description and pictures, see https://oi.uchicago.edu/collections/photographic-archives/persepolis/harem-xerxes (accessed December 4, 2017).
5. Josef Wiesehöfer, *Ancient Persia: From 550 BC to 650 AD,* trans. Azizeh Azodi (London, UK: I. B. Tauris, 2001), 40–41.
6. The "who" in verse 6 could refer to either Mordecai or Kish. If it is Mordecai, this would make him over 100 years old by the time of the Esther narrative (around 480 BC). It is thus more likely that the "who" refers to Kish.

means "Myrtle"[7] but also sounds like "hidden" in Hebrew).[8] The dual names remind us of Daniel and his friends in Babylon. They also had foreign names that sounded like local gods. They were quite confrontational when it came to following local laws that contravened God's laws. Perhaps Esther's name hints that her resistance will be more covert.[9]

The king's edict was proclaimed, and Esther was gathered and taken into the king's harem (v. 8). Here she played the game very well, pleasing the eunuch in charge of the harem and winning his favor (vv. 8–9). Soon, she was advanced to the best place in the king's harem (v. 11). This reminds us of Joseph, who also won the favor of his masters in Egypt – Potiphar and the prison warden (Gen 39:1–23). In the Joseph narrative, it is clear that God's hand was behind Joseph's success. God is not mentioned in Esther, but the similarities in the Esther and Joseph narratives at least hint that God's hand was also behind Esther's success in the palace.

Being a member of the king's harem was not as glamorous as we might think. Once Esther was in the king's harem, she was a "captive," placed in the custody of a eunuch (v. 8). She had lost her freedom; there was no possibility of escape. In a sense, she was a double captive and a victim of her circumstances. God's people, including Mordecai and Esther's ancestors, were also "carried away" as captives by the Babylonian king, Nebuchadnezzar (v. 6; 2 Kgs 25:1–21).[10] Esther had no control over what happened to her ancestors, especially their disobedience that led to their exile in Persia (Deut 28:63–64).

King Cyrus had issued a decree allowing the Jews to return to the Promised Land at least fifty years before the time of King Xerxes (2 Chr 36:22–23). Esther's ancestors in exile could have returned "home," but they had chosen not to. If her ancestors or she had returned home, which was further away from Susa, it might have been easier to evade the king's net. Back in the Promised Land she might have been less likely to find herself in her current predicament.

At times, we might think that we are victims of circumstance or of other peoples' decisions and actions. Yet we should gain hope in knowing that God

---

7. See, for example, Isa 41:19; Neh 8:15.
8. In the Esther narrative, she is only referred to as "Hadassah" in this verse; in the rest of the narrative she is known as "Esther."
9. Samuel Wells and George R. Sumner, *Esther & Daniel*, Brazos Theological Commentary on the Bible (Grand Rapids, MI: Brazos Press, 2013), 37. Some also find an allusion to God hiding in Esther's name; e.g., Leslie C. Allen and Timothy S. Laniak, *Ezra, Nehemiah, Esther* (Peabody, MA: Hendrickson, 2003), 206.
10. Different forms of *galah*, the Hebrew word for "carried away" or "removed," were used four times in Esth 2:6 to emphasize this point.

delivered his people from foreign bondage (vv. 5–7). Although Mordecai's ancestors had been taken as captives to Babylon, we know that the Jews were allowed to return to the Promised Land. Knowing that God uses every situation for the good of those who love him gives us hope (Rom 8:28–30). We can trust God in all circumstances because he is ever-faithful to his covenant people.

2:12–14 SCENE 2: A WOMAN'S TURN

In popular presentations of the book of Esther, the competition to select a new queen is commonly presented as a beauty pageant. Something like a Miss Asia competition. In recent years, the Philippines have been especially successful in global beauty pageants. Contestants need to train for at least six months before the competition, working on how to walk, how to do their hair and make-up, exercising, and learning how to answer questions.[11] Esther was involved in a competition also, but there are some significant differences. Just as in getting ready to compete in beauty pageants, the preparation period here was long. Before a "contestant" even went to the king, her beauty treatments lasted a whole year. She was prepared for six months with oil of myrrh and six months with perfumes and cosmetics. After these extravagant preparations, each woman had her "turn" to be with King Xerxes (v. 12). Then she was allowed to take whatever she wanted into the king's bedroom to please him (v. 13). It was not specified what she might bring in. Perhaps it might have been some food or wine that the king particularly liked; perhaps she might have brought in some aphrodisiacs. In any case, she had one night to satisfy the king in his bed, and then in the morning she would return to be part of his harem, as a concubine (v. 14).[12] Unless, of course, she was the one chosen to be queen.

Try to put yourself in the place of a "contestant." After your night with the king, you've now lost your "innocence"; you're now stuck in the king's service; you do not get to go home again; you do not get to marry anyone else. And unless you pleased the king, he will not call you back on another night. The women in the Persian Empire were treated as objects for the king's pleasure. They were used for his entertainment, then disposed of until he fancied them again – if he ever did (v. 14).

---

11. Amee Enriquez, "Philippines: How to Make a Beauty Queen," in *BBC News,* 2014, available online at http://www.bbc.com/news/world-asia-25550425 (accessed October 2, 2017).
12. Different forms of the verb *bo* are used five times in vv. 12–14, to describe "going to" or "going in to" King Xerxes. This word has a double meaning in Hebrew, denoting both movement from one place to another, and sexual activity (e.g., Judg 15:1).

But before you think the Persian practices were sexist, notice that males did not get away untouched, either. King Xerxes had the power to conscript them into his service also. After some "modification" they became eunuchs in his service, like Hegai and Shaashgaz. As eunuchs, they posed less threat to the king, and they were less likely to molest his harem of women. Would you rather have been a male or a female in the Persian Empire?

The king in ancient West Asia was meant to maintain justice, but unfortunately, the misuse of power was commonplace. This is the description of the king's role by King Darius I (father of Xerxes, who reigned 522–486 BC), written on one of his two epitaphs:

> By the favor of Ahura Mazda I am of such a sort that I am a friend to right, I am not a friend to wrong. It is not my desire that the weak man should have wrong done to him by the mighty; nor is it my desire that the mighty man should have wrong done to him by the weak. What is right, that is my desire.[13]

Similarly, the Israelite kings were to maintain justice, as we see in these verses ascribed to King Solomon:

> Endow the king with your justice, O God,
>   the royal son with your righteousness.
> May he judge your people in righteousness,
>   your afflicted ones with justice. (Ps 72:1–2)

Misuse of power and injustice is not just found with Persian kings. The prophet Samuel forewarned Israel that its kings would take their sons and daughters, fields and grain, and cattle and flocks (1 Sam 8:11–18). This became a reality in Israelite history, starting with King Solomon (e.g., 1 Kgs 5:13–17).

Yet not all kings abuse their power for their own pleasure. In the OT, there was also a search for a companion for King David. In his old age, David's servants also advised him to find a young virgin to wait upon him, be in his service, to lie in his arms, and to keep him warm (1 Kgs 1:2). Despite the similarities with King Xerxes' situation, there are significant differences. David's servants selected Abishag the Shunammite from throughout the land of Israel (1 Kgs 1:3); there was no group of women gathered into his harem for a contest (Esth 2:3). So, the choice of replacement for Vashti could have

---

13. Wiesehöfer, *Ancient Persia*, 33.

been done differently.[14] As we move to the New Testament, there would be another king who does not treat his people as objects (Phil 2:5–11).

2:15–18 SCENE 3: ESTHER WAS CHOSEN AS THE NEW QUEEN

We have reached the exciting point of the story when it was Esther's turn to go to the king (v. 15). She asked for nothing except what Hegai suggested she take with her. As someone who worked for the king, Hegai would have known best what would please the king. So, although some suggest that Esther was either indifferent to her circumstances or was submissive, her actions can also be seen as shrewd or wise.[15] Perhaps taking less than what the other girls brought made Esther stand out by contrast.

It was the seventh year of King Xerxes' reign (v. 16); that is, about four years after Queen Vashti had been deposed. In those four years, most scholars think that King Xerxes went to wage an unsuccessful war against Greece.[16] Now he was back. What was going to be his verdict?

Esther "won"! After her one night with the king, he found her more attractive than any of the other young women. Literally, "the king loved (*ahev*) Esther more than all the women." She had gained the favor and grace of Hegai and everyone else previously; so it was not surprising that she gained the king's approval.[17] The crown that had belonged to Vashti was now placed on Esther's head (v. 17). We do not know the depth or durability of the king's "love" for Esther, but for now, we can celebrate with King Xerxes. He threw another great feast, this one in Esther's honor. He also proclaimed a public holiday (NIV, NRSV) or a remission of taxes (ESV, NJPS)[18] and he generously handed out gifts to everyone (v. 18).

Yet as we watch and cheer for Esther's rise from a nobody to queen, we might feel a sense of discomfort. There is a Malay proverb: *masuk kandang kambing mengembek, masuk kandang kerbau menguak* ("when you enter the

---

14. Also in contrast to King Xerxes, King David had "no intimate relations" with Abishag (1 Kgs 1:4).
15. See Angeline Song, "Heartless Bimbo or Subversive Role Model?: A Narrative (Self) Critical Reading of the Character of Esther," *Dialog* 49 (2010): 59.
16. E.g., David J. A. Clines, *Ezra, Nehemiah, Esther*, NCBC (Grand Rapids: Eerdmans, 1984), 260–261. This reading is consistent with the historical sources.
17. Esther won the *hesedh* of Hegai (2:9) and the *hen* of "all who saw her" (2:15). She gained both the *hen* and the *hesedh* of the king (2:17). Esther reminds us of Ruth, who won the favor of Boaz (*hen*; Ruth 2:10, 13), as well as all the townspeople (Ruth 3:11).
18. Literally, *hanahah* means "a giving of rest," which could refer to either a release from work (a holiday) or a release from taxes (remission of taxes). See BDB, 629; *HALOT*, 82.

goat's pen, bleat; when you enter the water buffalo's pen, low"). It is best to abide by the customs of a society in which you are a visitor or resident. But had Esther gone too far? Her different names hint at the possibility of her switching between one identity and another. Mordecai forbade her from making known her Jewish identity (vv. 10, 20), and we wonder how much she might have compromised to get ahead in this worldly Persian kingdom. How many of the Old Testament laws did she not keep? Did she break the food laws? Did she rest on the Sabbath? This sense of discomfort was also felt by the Greek translators of the book of Esther. In the Septuagint, the Greek translation of the Old Testament, Esther stated that she has not violated the food laws, and that she abhorred "the bed of the uncircumcised" king.[19]

Certainly, from the narrative we can see that belonging to God's people must be dangerous, or at least disadvantageous, in some way. But did she compromise too much to keep her family background and ethnicity hidden?[20] After all, she went along with the contest, and did so well that she ended up marrying a foreign, pagan king.

Then we look at Vashti, who refused to go along with the empire. And we wonder if Esther also could have or should have refused to play the game. But it is hard for us to judge her because who knows what we would have done in her situation?

What we do know is that Esther's life is true to life. Her dilemma is similar to what we experience in our lives. We face the challenge of not hiding or compromising our faith to avoid problems. We face the difficult task of being in this world but not of this world.

Some people in Asia have accepted Jesus as their Lord and Savior but remain within their socio-religious communities, be it Islamic, Hindu, Buddhist, Jewish, or other. These followers of Jesus may hide their Christian identity for fear of persecution or even their lives.[21] Other Christians in Asia openly confess their faith and make a clear separation from their previous socio-religious practices. Often, this will also mean removing themselves from their former communities. The path chosen will require much prayer, wisdom, and discernment. The Apostle Paul tells us that all things are lawful but not

---

19. Addition C:26.
20. Carey A. Moore, *Esther,* AB 7B (Garden City: Doubleday, 1971), 28, comments: "In order for Esther to have concealed her ethnic and religious identity . . . in the harem, she must have eaten . . . , dressed, and lived like a Persian rather than an observant Jewess."
21. Following the example of Paul (1 Cor 9:19–23), among other reasons, other Christians living in Asia take on the socio-religious customs of local communities in order to share the gospel.

all are beneficial (1 Cor 10:23–33). Care, however, needs to be taken that the core beliefs of the Christian faith are not compromised. Paul was also strongly against those who distort the gospel (Gal 1:6–7), because salvation is at stake.

Others of us might be tempted to hide our Christian faith for our own advantage. One example may be to gain a promotion at work. Or we might be tempted to compromise our faith to be accepted by our friends. Yet, as Vashti shows us, we can say "No" to the kingdom of the world, but resisting may cost us our position in the world.

Sometimes saying "no" is essential. As James warns us, "You adulterous people, do not you know that friendship with the world means enmity against God? Therefore, anyone who chooses to be a friend of the world becomes an enemy of God" (Jas 4:4).

2:19–23 SCENE 4: MORDECAI FOILED A PLOT

In this scene we find there was more unrest in King Xerxes' kingdom. On the surface there were banquets and drinking, silver and sparkling jewels, but there was a darker underbelly. Not everyone living under the king was happy. Two eunuchs had murder on their minds (v. 21).

Our attention, though, is drawn to Mordecai. As Esther's cousin and guardian, he paced around anxiously in the courtyard near the harem to learn what was happening to Esther (v. 11). Now, when the virgins were assembled a second time, we find him seated at the king's gate (v. 19).[22] Excavations at Susa have uncovered a monumental gate to the east of the king's palace. It was 40m x 30m, and consisted of a central hall with four columns, with two rectangular side rooms.[23] In other words, this gate was a large building, very different from the gates that we commonly find in modern-day Asia. The king's gate contained rooms where people made legal and administrative decisions (elsewhere in the Bible, see Ruth 4:1–12; 2 Sam 15:2–6).[24] If the material remains from the excavation have been interpreted correctly, the monumental

---

22. It is not clear what this second gathering of virgins was. Since they are described as "virgins" (not a "concubine," 2:14), they could have been the unsuccessful contestants, who were about to be sent home; so Robert Gordis, "Studies in the Esther Narrative," *JBL* 95 (1976): 47. For a discussion of possibilities, see Frederic W. Bush, *Ruth, Esther*, WBC 9 (Dallas: Word Books, 1996), 371–372.

23. Prudence Oliver Harper, Joan Aruz, and Françoise Tallon, *The Royal City of Susa: Ancient Near Eastern Treasures in the Louvre* (New York: Metropolitan Museum of Art, 1992), 216. For an artist's reconstruction of the gate, see Edwin M. Yamauchi, *Persia and the Bible* (Grand Rapids, MI: Baker Book House, 1996), 299.

24. For a description of the Persian gates, with references, see Bush, *Ruth*, 372–373.

gate could be the one at which Mordecai was sitting. As such, Mordecai held an administrative position in the king's court, probably low-level.[25]

While at the gate, Mordecai heard of the assassination plot by two of the king's eunuchs (v. 22). We do not know why Bigthan and Teresh conspired against King Xerxes. They were meant to guard the "doorway" (NIV) or the "threshold" (ESV) just like security guards who restrict access to buildings today. That they would turn against the king was thus a serious security breach, with a good chance of success. King Xerxes was actually murdered in 465 BC by court officials, including the chief of his guards, Artapanus, and King Artaxerxes III (425–338 BC) was murdered by a eunuch. Thankfully for King Xerxes, Mordecai managed to foil the eunuchs' conspiracy by reporting their plot to Queen Esther. She reported it to King Xerxes, "in the name of Mordecai" – that is, she gave the credit to Mordecai. He saved the king's life, and the eunuchs were impaled on a pole as punishment and as deterrent.

It was all recorded in the official Persian historical annals, but for some reason, King Xerxes forgot what Mordecai had done (v. 23). Mordecai was not rewarded as he should have been. But there is another king who does not forget. As we will find out later in the story of Esther, God used this seemingly forgotten footnote of history for greater purposes.

In this scene, we find Mordecai going about his usual business, working as an official in the Persian government. He was a member of a minority ethnic and religious group within Persian society. Although there was a lurking danger in being a member of God's people, Mordecai still sought to promote the good of the government for which he worked. In this way, his actions were consistent with the Prophet Jeremiah's advice, to "seek the peace and prosperity of the city to which I have carried you into exile" (Jer 29:7). Flourishing for the city meant flourishing for those who live in it, including the Jews.

Nonetheless, we too might not always receive immediate recognition for our work. For instance, Ferdinand Kittel was a missionary to India, arriving in 1853. He served in south India, where he strove to learn the Kannada language, customs, and music. In his native Germany, he was marginalized by the Basel Church Mission because of his missionary techniques. Today in Germany, he is all but forgotten. In Karnataka, however, he is widely known for his work on revising the Kannada Bible and especially for producing a Kannada-English dictionary. Educational institutions are named after him, as well as roads and

---

25. A high-ranking position was unlikely, since his refusal to bow down to Haman went unnoticed for a long time (3:1–4); Michael V. Fox, *Character and Ideology in the Book of Esther* (Columbia, SC: University of South Carolina Press, 1991), 42.

even a town in Bangalore.[26] Similarly, our work might not be recognized in our lifetime or even at all. Yet we continue to serve in a way that others might see our good works and give glory to our Father in heaven (Matt 5:16).

WORKING FOR THE KING

Those of us living in Asia under an oppressive government can take comfort in the Esther narrative. As we observe the people of God in Esther 2, we might find that there is no one correct response to an oppressive regime. The two Jews in this chapter responded in different ways to their situations. Esther can be seen as someone who submitted to the empire, who played along with the "contest" and became King Xerxes' next queen. Yet the way in which she won the favor of everyone with whom she was in contact within the palace hints at her superior ability in "playing the game." Our suspicion is confirmed in her decision to follow the advice of Hegai as she entered the king's bedroom for her night with King Xerxes.

The second Jew in Esther 2, Mordecai, can be seen to actively support the Persian Empire. When he received inside information that the king's life was in danger, he acted quickly and decisively to thwart the threat. As a member of a minority group in the Persian Empire, he might have been tempted to band together with the rebellious eunuchs. However, he wisely chose to protect the king instead. Certainly, it was a generally peaceful time in the Persian realm; it seems there was no overt threat to the Jews as long as they laid low.

One of the difficulties of the Esther narrative is that the narrator did not give us any clear advice about how we should live in the face of an oppressive government. Many of us in Asia might prefer to distill "three things we should do this week" from a Bible passage. However, the Esther narrative (and much of the OT narrative) is firmly resistant to producing such easy moral lessons. Did Esther make the right decision to "play the game" well? Should she have competed half-heartedly, in a passive-resistant way, so she would not have been successful in the king's contest to find a queen? Should Mordecai have returned to build his life in Jerusalem instead of helping to build up the Persian Empire?

Just like the characters in the Esther narrative, we do not have easy answers to these questions and dilemmas. However, we can empathize with them, knowing that this is how life often is for us as well. At times, there are

---

26. For more detail, see Reinhard Wendt, ed., *An Indian to the Indians?: On the Initial Failure and Posthumous Success of the Missionary Ferdinand Kittel, 1832–1903* (Wiesbaden, Germany: Harrassowitz Verlag, 2006).

clear black and white moral decisions we need to make – right or wrong – but often we must live life and make decisions in morally gray circumstances. So, we pray earnestly for God's wisdom to make the best decision in the situation in which God has placed us with the information available to us.

The comfort for us is that we can leave the outcome of our decisions to God, trusting that he will remain faithful to us, because he is a covenant-keeping God. He delivered his people Israel from bondage in Egypt; he delivered his people from bondage in Babylon. He delivered us from bondage to Satan, sin, and death through Jesus, and we look forward to our ultimate deliverance when Jesus returns. God is always looking out for our best interests (Rom 8:28–29) and seeking to work for his glory. Even in our "day jobs" he is the hidden king for whom we work with all our hearts (Col 3:23–24).

ESTHER 3

Living in this world can be dangerous if you are a member of God's people. Living in Asia, I have met followers of Jesus Christ who were formerly from the majority religion of their country. They need to meet secretly in house-churches for fear of punishment or even in fear for their lives. In one church my family and I attended, there was a girl who had fled a West Asian country because of persecution. If she returned home her family would kill her because they hated the fact that she had become a Christian. There are also many refugees in Asia who have been displaced from their own countries because of persecution for their Christian faith.

As we turn to Esther 3, we find that the simmering danger for the people of God in chapter 2 now becomes outright conflict and threat. Chapter 3 is similar to chapter 1 because both involve conflict. The major conflict of Esther 1 was between King Xerxes and Queen Vashti. She refused to respect the king's wishes; she was punished with expulsion, and a decree was dispatched. In Esther 3 we find another conflict, this time between the king's Prime Minister and the Jews, the people of God in the post-exilic OT period. Mordecai the Jew refused to show respect to Haman, but the matter quickly escalated from a personal conflict to include a whole group of people, the Jews. Similar to Esther 1, by the end of the chapter another decree was dispatched to every corner of the Persian Empire, but this decree had much more destructive potential than the first one.

In this chapter, we first examine how Mordecai angered Haman (vv. 1–6). Then we look at how Haman hoodwinked King Xerxes into agreeing to his plan of annihilation (vv. 7–11). The final scene describes how Haman's edict was dispatched (vv. 12–15). We will then consider the theme of the suffering of God's people within the Bible. As we do so, we will find that we can gain encouragement in our being persecuted when we view it within the overarching storyline of the whole Bible.

3:1–6 SCENE 1: MORDECAI ANGERED HAMAN

Mordecai had just foiled an assassination plot (2:19–23), but we do not find that he had been promoted as we might expect. Haman was promoted instead; part of this involved him being given "a seat of honor higher than that of all the other nobles" (v. 1). This was the Greek historian Xenophon's description of Cyrus's (king prior to Xerxes) giving of public recognition: "He did not, however, assign the appointed place permanently, but he made it a rule that by noble deeds any one might advance to a more honored seat, and that if anyone should conduct himself ill he should go back to one less honored."[1] If this was the case, Haman's place of honor was thus not secure. So we can understand some of Haman's insecurity later in the Esther narrative, as expressed in his need for public adoration.[2]

Haman's promotion took place about five years after Mordecai had saved the king's life. In the events of the narrative, however, Haman's promotion happened straight after the failed coup. The Persians were known for awarding those who were loyal to the empire, but what had Haman done?[3] If the promotion was a result of the attempted coup, then King Xerxes may have been reshuffling his leadership and selecting leaders whom he could trust, including Haman.[4] Since the reason for the promotion was not given, we cannot be certain.

Immediately after Haman's promotion the tension grew. King Xerxes "commanded" his servants at the gate to bow down and pay homage to Haman. If this "command" (tsavah) was a personal initiative of King Xerxes, instead of an official Persian edict as found elsewhere in Esther (dath or dabar),[5] then this type of command might suggest that bowing to Haman did not come naturally. The Greek historian Herodotus described how Persians of different social levels normally greeted each other. If they were of the same social level, they kissed on the lips. If one was from a slightly lower level, they kissed on the cheeks. If one was "inferior by a long way, he [fell] to the ground and prostrate[d] himself in front of the other person."[6] If bowing down was the general Persian custom, it would have been expected that people would have normally bowed down to Haman. For the king to command obeisance suggests that people might not have liked or naturally respected Haman.[7]

In any case, Mordecai did not follow the king's command (v. 2), although he was willing to obey the king previously (2:19–23). Why not? The Old Testament law did not forbid Mordecai from bowing. Paying respect

1. *Cyropaedia* 8.4.5, which was written around 370 BC.
2. Adele Berlin, *Esther* (Philadephia, PA: Jewish Publication Society, 2001), 34.
3. E.g., Herodotus 3.154.1: "For good service among the Persians is very much esteemed, and rewarded by high preferment."
4. Tod Linafelt and Timothy K. Beal, *Ruth & Esther*, Berit Olam (Collegeville, MN: Liturgical Press, 1999), 44–45.
5. Linda M. Day, *Esther*, Abingdon Old Testament Commentaries (Nashville, TN: Abingdon Press, 2005), 67.
6. Herodotus 1.134.1.
7. Joyce G. Baldwin, *Esther*, TOTC (Leicester, UK: InterVarsity Press, 1984), 72.

to someone does not necessarily mean that you are treating them as a god. Elsewhere in the OT, God's people bowed down to those in authority (e.g., Gen 42:6; Exod 18:7; 1 Sam 24:9). On first glance, perhaps we think that maybe Mordecai just did not like Haman, or, maybe Mordecai was bitter that Haman had been promoted instead of him.

Anyway, the king's servants were as puzzled as we are about Mordecai's refusal to bow. So, they kept pestering him, and asked the question which is also on our minds: "Why do you disobey the king's command?" (v. 3). When Mordecai explained to them that it was because he was a Jew, they reported it to Haman "to see if [Mordecai's] behavior will be tolerated" (v. 4).[8] In any case, Haman became enraged, just like his king had been (1:12), and his reaction to Mordecai's disrespect was extreme. Once he learned that Mordecai was a Jew, killing him alone was not enough. Haman looked for a way to kill all of Mordecai's people (vv. 5–6). So Mordecai's disobedience put at risk the lives of all Jews in the whole Persian Empire.

Haman's proposal was something like "The Nine Kinship Exterminations" in ancient China. This was punishment for the most serious offences, such as treason. Not only was the offender killed but also nine different groups from the offender's family, such as parents, grandparents, children, cousins, and so on – up to nine different groups related to the offender. Hence, it was called "The Nine Kinship Exterminations." However, Haman's retaliation against Mordecai was even worse. He not only wanted to wipe out Mordecai and nine groups of Mordecai's family, he sought to destroy Mordecai's whole people, the Jews. There are many unanswered questions from the narrative. Why was there such an extreme response from Haman? Was it just because Mordecai refused to bow down to him? Perhaps Haman thought that if one Jew would not bow to him, the rest of them would not either. Even then his response still seems too extreme. There must have been something else also motivating him, and for Mordecai, was there a deeper reason why he refused to bow to Haman?

A closer look at the Bible text suggests a reason: their family backgrounds. Haman was described as an Agagite (v. 1). The narrator repeated this description of Haman later in the chapter, when it was not strictly necessary (v. 10), as if to emphasize Haman's background. Agag was the Amalekite king who was spared by King Saul. Saul's refusal to obey God by executing King Agag was a major factor that cost Saul his kingship (see 1 Sam 15). Mordecai was a Jew,

---

8. For the similarities between this passage and Joseph's refusal to yield to Potiphar's wife (especially between Esth 3:4 and Gen 39:10), see Jon D. Levenson, *Esther*, OTL (Louisville, KY: Westminster John Knox, 1997), 68.

and that was the reason he gave for refusing to bow to Haman (v. 4). He was from the tribe of Benjamin, the same tribe as Saul. One of his ancestors was Kish, Saul's father (2:5). Thus, the Esther narrative points to an underlying bitterness between Haman's ancestors and Mordecai's ancestors as the cause for Mordecai's refusal.

A comparison with the Greek Additions to the scroll of Esther brings this out further. In Addition C, Mordecai prayed to God about his actions, stating that he did not refuse to pay homage because of pride. He said, "But I did this so that I might not set human glory above the glory of God, and I will not bow down to anyone but you" (vv. 5–7). Furthermore, the Greek versions of Esther (LXX, AT) did not mention Haman's Amalekite ancestry. Instead, they called him "the Bougean" or "the Macedonian," descriptors that would be pejorative during a time of Hellenistic threat. By contrast, then, Mordecai and Haman's ancestral backgrounds stand out in the OT text (MT) as likely reasons for Mordecai's refusal to pay homage.

However, the hatred goes back even further than just a few generations. When Israel was travelling through the wilderness on the way to Mt. Sinai, the Amalekites came out to fight against Israel (see Exod 17). So, the bitterness was also between Haman's people and Mordecai's people. Indeed, God had commanded that Israel "blot out" the name of Amalek (Deut 25:19). The Targums expanded the hostility back even further, by extending Haman's ancestry to Esau (Gen 36:12), thus invoking the rivalry between Jacob and Esau.[9]

Thus, Mordecai did not transgress the king's command because he was being disloyal to the king. His refusal was not primarily out of arrogance or because of a personal conflict with Haman. Rather, hints in the Esther narrative and reading within the sweep of the OT suggest that his disobedience was because of a long-standing feud between his people and Haman's people. Mordecai was representative of the Jews (v. 4), just as Haman was a representative "enemy of the Jews" (v. 10). A Jew could not bow down to an Amalekite. Mordecai took a stand based on principle, which led him to break Persian law.

If this is the case, then there is an echo of this in the NT. Peter and the Apostles refused to obey human authorities when their rules clashed with God's commands (see Acts 5:27–29). In Malaysia, a recent high-profile case of Christians challenging the government was in regard to the use of the word "Allah." Christians have used the word "Allah" to refer to "God" in their Malay language Bibles and publications since before the creation of the Malaysian

---

9. Berlin, *Esther*, 34.

nation. Yet on December 10, 2007, the Ministry of Home Affairs ordered the weekly Catholic newsletter, the *Herald*, not to use the word "Allah" in its Malay language publication. Other clashes between government authorities and Protestant Christian groups over the usage of "Allah" have followed. Many Malaysian Christians agreed that they must stand up to this government ruling.[10] There have been legal challenges, and the issue is still ongoing. In our lives, individually and corporately, there may be situations where we need to take a stand based on our Christian principles.

3:7–11 SCENE 2: HAMAN HOODWINKED XERXES

As the next scene begins we see that Haman cast lots (or *pur*). *Pur* is an Akkadian word meaning stone, and casting lots in ancient Mesopotamia was done by casting a small stone die.[11] In the OT, lots (*goral*) were also cast. God commanded the use of lots for the two goats on the Day of Atonement (Lev 16:5–10); lots were cast for assigning inheritance (Josh 18–19) and to identify transgressors.[12] They were also cast to determine war strategy (Judg 20:9) and the divisions for priestly service (1 Chr 24:1–18). Moreover, lots were used to select Saul as the first king (1 Sam 10:19–21). Yet proverbial wisdom is that God decides the outcome of the cast lots (Prov 16:33).[13]

In the Esther narrative, Haman was superstitious and wanted to find the most auspicious date for his scheme (v. 7). He too had a hunch that the date was determined by a greater power. This was not mentioned in the MT but was described in the AT: "So Haman went to his gods to learn the day of their death and cast lots" (AT 3:7). This is similar to thinking in Chinese culture, whereby some people try to have their children born in an auspicious year. Some Chinese couples consult the Chinese calendar to find the most favorable date to marry. In Malaysia sometimes mediums are consulted to determine dates and years.[14] Haman probably used an astrologer to cast the lot for the most auspicious month for his planned scheme.

10. Not all Christians agree. Some would prefer to stop using the word "Allah" altogether, since it has strong associations with the Islamic god.
11. The casting of lots by the Persians was noted by the Greek historians, e.g., Herodotus 3.128; Xenophon, *Cyropaedia* 1.6.46.
12. Some examples include Achan, Jonah, and Jonathan (Josh 7; Jonah 1:4–7; 1 Sam 14:41–43).
13. Lots continued to be used in the NT. It was the way in which Zechariah was chosen to burn incense in the temple, Judas' replacement was chosen, and Jesus' garments were divided up at his crucifixion (Luke 1:9; Acts 1:15–26; John 19:24).
14. See, e.g., Raymond L. M. Lee, "Continuity and Change in Chinese Spirit Mediumship in Urban Malaysia," *Bijdragen tot de Taal-, Land-en Volkenkunde* 142 (1986): 203.

With the date set, Haman approached the king with his request. Haman was masterful in his use of words in persuading the king to accept his request. His approach reminds us of the serpent's shrewd tactics in the Garden of Eden (Gen 3:1–5): he began his speech with truths that he twisted into half-truths and then ended with an outright lie (v. 8).

It is true that there was a "certain people" (nameless and hence without distinct identity) dispersed among the peoples in the Persian Empire. However, in describing the Jews as those who "keep themselves separate," Haman was saying that the Jews were not assimilated into Persian society. We know this was not true, at least for the Jews in the Esther narrative so far. Other OT books describing Jews in the diaspora give us a fuller picture of the degree of assimilation of the Jews. Although Daniel and his friends willingly worked for foreign kings, they were presented as less assimilated than Mordecai and Esther. Ezra and Nehemiah also worked for foreign kings but were also concerned for their fellow Jews in the Promised Land. However, Mordecai needed to reveal that he was a Jew to the king's servants at the gate (v. 4), and Esther was so well assimilated that no one in the palace knew her ethnic background either, not even her husband, the king.

It was true that "their customs [were] different" because the Jews were the sole recipients of the Torah, the OT Law (see Deut 4:8). However, we also know that in order to follow the customs in the king's palace, Esther must have broken OT Law. For instance, she married a foreigner, and she most likely ate defiled food (in contrast with Daniel and his friends in Daniel 1).

Finally, it was untrue that the Jews did "not obey the king's laws," because in the narrative so far, we have witnessed at least two from this ethnic group who have submitted to Persian law. Mordecai had just saved the king's life, in contrast to the treasonous acts of the eunuchs. Of course, it is true that Mordecai disobeyed the king's "command" to bow to Haman, but technically, this was not one of the king's laws. Furthermore, in a similar sense, Esther also "obeyed" the king by coming to his palace to be selected as queen. Thus, it is a lie that it was "not in the king's best interest to tolerate them," especially since we have just witnessed Mordecai saving the king's life (2:19–23). Haman literally says, "It is not to the king's best interest to *cause them to rest* (*lehanniham*)." This lack of rest (*nuakh*, the same root word) for the Jews anticipated and contrasted with the rest that they would enjoy by the end of the narrative (9:16, 17, 18, 22).

As we briefly considered above, it may be that Haman's accusations were correct, and Mordecai and Esther were exceptions. Perhaps the rest of the Jews did live separately, keeping the Jewish laws and not keeping the king's laws. From the king's perspective, perhaps these were indications that the Jews were not loyal subjects of the Persian Empire. Yet, so far in the Esther narrative, Mordecai and Esther were the only Jews who have been introduced. Moreover, they were portrayed as representatives of their people, the Jews. Because of Mordecai's refusal to bow, all the Jews were under Haman's edict. As we will see in the next chapter, Mordecai led his people in mourning, and Esther made a decision that impacted all the Jews. It was rare that people would follow leaders who were markedly dissimilar to themselves.[15] Also, it seems unlikely that the author of Esther would portray the main characters in a way in which the original audience would not identify. It seems more likely, then, that Mordecai and Esther were not just representatives of the Jews; they were representative of the Jews.

Historical sources indicate that significant anti-Jewish sentiment only arose after the Persian Period. During the Hellenistic period, antagonism towards Jews was particularly intense, especially under the Seleucid Empire (c. 200 BC), leading to the Maccabean revolts (167–164 BC). King Cyrus was known for his tolerance of the religions and cultures of his conquered peoples (e.g., 2 Chr 36:22–23; Ezra 1:1–4), and it seems King Xerxes continued this policy.[16] The only evidence that King Xerxes was intolerant of foreign deities was when the peoples who worshiped those deities were not loyal to him.[17] Hellenistic rulers, by contrast, sought for ancestral practices to be abandoned, a policy that led to hostility towards the Jews. Given this information, even if the Jews were not assimilated, as Haman argues, it seems this was more a personal issue for him than a general Persian stance.

To increase the likelihood of the success of his proposal to King Xerxes, Haman threw in a massive bribe of 10,000 talents (about 330 tons) of silver (v. 9). Giving money to win a contract is not just something that is done today. Haman's bribe was a huge sum – estimated to be equivalent to over two-thirds of the yearly tax revenue of the whole Persian Empire.[18] Since it

---

15. S. Alexander Haslam, Stephen Reicher, and Michael Platow, *The New Psychology of Leadership: Identity, Influence, and Power* (Hove, UK: Psychology Press, 2011).

16. For pictures of the Cyrus Cylinder and a translation, see http://britishmuseum.org/research/collection_online/collection_object_details.aspx?objectId=327188&partId=1 (accessed December 5, 2017).

17. For a balanced comparison of King Cyrus and King Xerxes' reigns, see Josef Wiesehöfer, *Ancient Persia: From 550 BC to 650 AD*, trans. Azizeh Azodi (London, UK: I. B. Tauris, 2001), 42–55.

18. Lewis B. Paton, *A Critical and Exegetical Commentary on the Book of Esther* (Edinburgh, UK: T&T Clark, 1976), 205. Frederic W. Bush, *Ruth, Esther*, WBC 9 (Dallas, TX: Word

is unimaginable that this amount would be paid out of Haman's personal wealth, maybe he thought he could seize this much from the Jews after he destroyed them. In any case, this huge sum reflected just how much Haman hated the Jews. Thus, in this shrewd way, Haman fooled King Xerxes into agreeing to annihilate God's people. The deal was then sealed (vv. 10–11) without the king even having enquired about the identity of this unnamed group of people.

There is a Malay proverb that goes, *Gajah berjuang sama gajah, pelanduk mati di tengah-tengah.* ("When elephants clash, mouse-deer die underfoot.") When kings fight, the citizens suffer. The king handed over his signet ring as a symbol of his authority along with the money and the Jews for Haman to "do with the people as [he] pleased." "Keep the money" (NIV) is literally "the silver is given to you," by which the king accepted the money but made it available for Haman to use.[19] Of course, handing over the Jews to Haman to do what was good in his eyes was ominous, for he was now unmasked as the "enemy of the Jews." As if to reinforce to a Jewish reader who Haman was and what he was capable of, his full titles were repeated: "the Agagite, the son of Hammedatha" (v. 10). What pleased Haman would be disastrous for the Jews.

3:12–15 SCENE 3: HAMAN'S EDICT WAS DISPATCHED

Royal secretaries were summoned, and under Haman's command they transcribed his edict. The edict was written to every level of Persian hierarchy – the king's satraps, the governors of the provinces, and the nobles of all the peoples (v. 12). The edict aimed to "destroy, kill and annihilate all the Jews – young and old, women and children – on a single day" (v. 13). The use of three words with similar meanings (kill, destroy, annihilate) underlined the totality of the genocide. Even as we read it today, the ruthlessness of this holocaust is enough to send a chill down our spines.

The edict was dispatched by royal mail to every corner of the Persian Empire (v. 14). Just as with the first edict which enforced women to respect their husbands, this edict was sent out to every province in its own script and every people in their own language (vv. 12–13; compare 1:22). There was a stark contrast in the people's response to this new edict: the king and Haman celebrated with wine, but the people were bewildered and confused (v. 15).

Books, 1996), 382, estimates it was a full year's revenue.
19. That the king accepted the silver was mentioned by Mordecai (4:7) and was also consistent with Esther describing the Jews as being "sold" (7:4).

Those behind the decree were callously ignorant of the effect that their decree would have on all the people affected by it.

As Haman and the king sat down to enjoy their wine, we must step back from the narrative to consider: Was there another power at work behind the timing of this terrible edict? There are two hints that there was. First, the decree was written on the thirteenth day of the first month. This was a day before Passover. So, we wonder if there will be another deliverance like the Exodus? We might not take notice of the date unless we are Jewish, but this was a significant date – like the day before December 25. Second, the date that was set for the genocide was the thirteenth day of the twelfth month (v. 13). This was eleven months in the future. Remember that this date was set by Haman when he cast lots. We recall that Proverbs 16:33 says, "The lot is cast into the lap, but its every decision is from the LORD." Verse 14 says that the decree was proclaimed to "the people of every nationality so that they would be ready for that day." Again, we wonder: Could it be that a hidden hand set this date so that the Jews also had more time to be ready to respond to this decree? After all, if the date were set for an earlier month, it would have given the Jews less time to prepare.

Thus, God's hidden hand may be detected in these dates and months. Even so, Haman was still responsible for his evil intentions and actions (and, to a lesser degree, the king was also responsible because he had given power to Haman). In fact, God's plan will be carried out despite the actions of individuals. This is similar to what happened to Joseph. His brothers meant to harm him, "but God intended it for good to accomplish what is now being done, the saving of many lives" (Gen 50:20).

We can praise God that his purposes are always achieved. Even the actions of "wicked men" ultimately led to our salvation (Acts 2:22–23).

THE PERSECUTION CONTINUED

Unfortunately, hatred against God's people is not just limited to the time of Esther. It was present throughout Israel's history. The Pharaoh of Egypt tried to kill all the Israelite baby boys while Israel was outside the Promised Land (Exod 1:15–22). The Amalekites tried to wipe out the Israelites when they were on their way to Sinai (Exod 17:8–16). The Philistines and other nations attacked Israel in the Promised Land (e.g., 1 Sam 4, 17).

According to the NT, the people of God today are Christians. The Apostle Paul says that those who have faith in Jesus are the children of Abraham, heirs of God's promise (Gal 3:7, 29). At times, persecutors will use truths, half-truths and flat-out lies to incite the authorities against Christians. Jesus describes the devil as "a murderer from the beginning," who uses lies, since "he is a liar and the father of lies" (John 8:44). Slander was used against Jesus to kill him. Slander was used against Jesus' followers in Acts 17:6–7.

So sadly, Haman is not unique. Haman-types have slandered and tried to kill God's people throughout history. They will continue to do so today. There are many Asian nations in the Open Doors 2017 World Watchlist of countries where Christians are persecuted.[1] At the top of the list is North Korea, but other countries such as Pakistan (fourth), India (fifteenth), Vietnam (seventeenth), Malaysia (thirty-first) and China (thirty-ninth) are also on the list. No matter which country we live in, we know that Jesus has said that all Christians should expect persecution as part and parcel of following him (e.g., John 15:18–21). Indeed, the Apostle Paul tells us that all who seek to live a godly life in Christ Jesus will suffer persecution (2 Tim 3:10–15). While God's people escaped death at the hand of Haman, Christians in NT times and beyond have been martyred, e.g., Stephen (Acts 7:54–60, see also Rev 17:6).

Yet Jesus' words to the persecuted church in Smyrna can give us encouragement in our suffering for the sake of Christ. That church in the first century faced slander, imprisonment, and possible death because of their faith in Jesus (Rev 2:8–11). Jesus tells his church not to fear. Instead, if we find ourselves undergoing persecution, we are encouraged to persevere unto death. For Jesus himself died and then came back to life, and so he is able to give us the crown of (eternal) life as our reward for enduring persecution.

---

1. For the full list, see https://www.opendoorsusa.org/christian-persecution/world-watch-list/ (accessed February 6, 2017).

ESTHER 4

Unlike those living in some other parts of the world, in Asia we generally do not question whether there is a God or not. Instead, the question for us is, "Which God?" This is consistent with the worldview of the Bible, in which God is described as eternally existent (e.g., Ps 90:2) and present everywhere in his creation (e.g., 1 Kgs 8:27; Job 38–41; Ps 139; Jer 23:23–24; Amos 9:2–6). At times we may *feel* that he is absent, as his presence in person, word, or action might be concealed for a time. However, he is never completely absent.

So far in the book of Esther, God has not been mentioned. He is not mentioned in the rest of the book either. One effect of hiding God and his actions is that there is more emphasis on us: our actions, our initiatives, our courage in acting. In Esther 4 we will examine the actions of Mordecai and Esther.

The previous chapter ended with Haman's decree dispatched to every far-flung corner of the Persian Empire. The decree threw the people of the city of Susa into confusion. As Esther 4 begins, we see that Mordecai and the Jews were not only confused, they were in mourning (vv. 1–3). As Mordecai performed his mourning ritual in the city and at the king's gate he caught the attention of Esther, who was hidden away in her residence and isolated from the activities of the world. After Esther's maids and eunuchs informed her about what Mordecai was doing, they engaged in a discussion about what to do. The discussion went back and forth five times through a middleman, Hathak, although he receded to the background as the dialog develops:

1. Esther sent Hathak to find out why Mordecai was wailing and mourning (vv. 5–6)
2. Mordecai sent Hathak back to explain what had happened, with a copy of Haman's decree, and commanded her to plead with King Xerxes (vv. 7–9)
3. Esther sent Hathak to Mordecai to explain that she could not go to the king (vv. 10–12)
4. Mordecai told "them" to reply to Esther with further arguments to persuade her to go to the king (vv. 13–14)
5. Esther sent "them" to inform Mordecai that she would take action (vv. 15–16).

The use of the middleman highlights the physical and social distance between Mordecai and Esther. Yet this did not end up being a major barrier in their communication. The use of direct speech from step 3 to the end of the communication, along with the reduced direct mention of the middleman, brings a sense of growing intimacy and immediacy to their dialog.[1]

We will look at their dialog in two parts. Esther effectively informed Mordecai that she was reluctant to take any action (vv. 4–11), but ultimately Mordecai persuaded Esther to side with her people. The chapter ends when she courageously took the initiative to try to deliver them (vv. 12–17).

4:1–3 SCENE 1: THE JEWS MOURNED

The next scene shows the effect that the edict had on Mordecai and the Jews. When Mordecai "learned" (*yada*) of Haman's decree,[2] he tore his clothes, put on sackcloth and ashes, and then wailed loudly and bitterly in the middle of the city (v. 1).[3] Since he could have mourned in private or at least in a less conspicuous public location, this was a deliberate demonstration of his grief for all to see. His mourning at the king's gate also suggests that his actions were intermingled with a degree of protest against the decree. Mordecai, the one who had triggered the impending calamity, then led his people in a public display of grief. This brought attention to the plight of his people, and, as probably as intended, drew the attention of Esther, his cousin. Those of us in Asia are aware of how loud the wailing can be at funerals. In this scene, it was not only Mordecai who mourned but also all the Jews. So we can imagine how noisy it would have been.

But what was missing from the narrator's description of Mordecai's response? It was also missing in the response of the Jews in all the Persian Empire

---

1. The use of the third person plural pronoun instead of "Hathak" either denotes the presence of more than one messenger or the use of an "indirect subject"; see Bruce K. Waltke and Michael P. O'Connor, *An Introduction to Biblical Hebrew Syntax* (Winona Lake, IN: Eisenbrauns, 1990), § 4.4.2. Given the way the rest of the dialogue was presented by the narrator, the latter seems a better option. This is brought out in some translations, including the NIV (ESV in brackets for comparison): (1) "When Esther's words were reported to Mordecai" (v. 12; "And *they* told Mordecai what Esther had said"); (2) "He sent back this answer" (v. 13; "Then Mordecai told *them* to reply to Esther"); (3) "Then Esther sent this reply to Mordecai" (v. 15; "Then Esther told *them* to reply to Mordecai"). The receding of a minor character into the background can be viewed as a literary method; see Yonatan Grossman, "The Vanishing Character in Biblical Narrative: The Role of Hathach in Esther 4," *VT* 62 (2012): 561–571.
2. "To know" (*yada*) is a motif woven through this chapter (vv. 1, 5, 11, 14). Previously in the book of Esther, this same word was used in the "wise men" who "knew the times" (1:13). It was also used when Mordecai paced back and forth to "find out" how Esther was (2:11) and when he "found out" the plot (2:22).
3. For more information on the ritual of mourning within the context of the ancient Near East, see Roland de Vaux, *Ancient Israel: Its Life and Institutions,* trans. John McHugh; 2nd ed. (London, UK: Dartman Longman & Todd, 1965), 59.

(v. 3): prayer. Some commentators suggest that the Jews in Persia were God's people in name only and that they did not pray at all. Even if that were the case during the rest of their lives, at least in times of crisis we would expect them to turn to God in prayer. In our societies, even non-believers are known to pray to God when they are desperate! In the rest of the Bible, national crises usually led to mourning and fasting and often triggered repentance and prayer (e.g., Lam 3:40–66). This was the response of God's people in another Bible text set in the same historical period as the Esther narrative. In the time of Nehemiah, the people fasted and put on sackcloth, as well as prayed to God (Neh 9:1–5).[4] The enormity of the impending disaster probably prompted Mordecai and the Jews to repent and pray. The Greek Additions to the Esther scroll describe Mordecai as having pleaded with God to intervene on behalf of the Jews.[5] However, repentance and prayer are not mentioned in the MT, so the one to whom they turned is hidden.

The tendency to be God's people in name only is found throughout the Bible. Just like Esther and Mordecai, our lives may be so similar to those around us that non-believers cannot tell that we are members of God's people unless we reveal this to them. In the OT, God often needed to remind the Israelites to keep choosing to obey him (e.g., Deut 30:15–20). God reminded his people that they needed to pass on a fresh faith to the next generation (e.g., Deut 6:6–7, 20–25; Josh 4:21–24), otherwise knowledge of God and a relationship with him can be lost (e.g., Judg 2:10). As Christians, we need to make sure that we have a living, personal relationship with the Lord Jesus. We too need to make sure that we pass our faith on to the next generation (e.g., 2 Tim 3:14–17).

Mordecai was mourning at the king's gate (v. 2), but Esther was blissfully unaware of the things taking place outside her residence. In fact, it seems likely that Mordecai was expressing his grief publicly in order to catch Esther's attention. Large public protests in Asia are often held near places of power to gain the attention of those in charge. For instance, towards the end of South Korean Park Geun-hye's presidency there were massive rallies, one of which stretched from the City Hall to the old palace gate and near to the Blue House, the presidential office and residence. In the Esther narrative, the orphan and her guardian were only separated by a gate, but she might as well have been living in a different world.

---

4. See also 2 Sam 12:22; Jonah 3:5–9.
5. Addition C:1–10 (LXX).

4:4–11 SCENE 2: ESTHER'S RESISTANCE

Esther needed to be told by her attendants and eunuchs of Mordecai's predicament. When she was informed about Mordecai's wailing, she was "deeply distressed."[6] So perhaps she tried to soothe him by sending clothes (v. 4). This is like putting a small Band-aid on a large gaping wound! Her solution was not suitable because she had no idea what the problem was. Those in leadership positions need to be wary of becoming so remote from the general population that they do not know the needs of ordinary people.

Or perhaps Esther sent him clothes so that his attire would allow him access to the palace to speak with her face-to-face. In any case, he flatly refused her offer, perhaps because he felt his mourning had not run its course yet. So Esther sent her messenger to find out (literally, "to know" [*yada*]) the reason for Mordecai's unusual behavior (v. 5). She soon learned that Haman had issued a decree to destroy the Jews (vv. 6–8).

Indirectly, Mordecai informed her that he was responsible for the present crisis. He explained to her "everything that happened to him" (v. 7). His knowledge of the exact sum of money showed that he had access to intimate information inside the palace. By revealing the enormous sum of money, Mordecai underlined both the resolve of Haman and the enormity of the problem which faced Esther and her people.

With a copy of the decree, Mordecai had strong evidence of the threat to the Jews. He handed the written text to Hathak, Esther's assistant, to pass to her. Through Hathak, Mordecai "commanded" (*tsavah*)[7] Esther, "to go into the king's presence to beg for mercy and plead with him for her people" (v. 8). It was significant that Mordecai told her to plead "on behalf of her people" because this would have entailed Esther revealing her Jewish identity. Previously Mordecai had told Esther to hide that aspect of her identity (compare 2:10, 20). Now he urged her to beg with the king on the basis of her social identity as a Jew. Because she had concealed her social identity and had achieved so much because of it, Mordecai needed to work hard to persuade her that acting on the basis of her social identity was crucial.

This turned out to be the case. Esther's first response was to resist Mordecai's command. She gave him three reasons why she could not go to plead with the king (v. 11): (1) It was against the law; (2) she would die if she broke the law; and (3) she was not favored by the king. She said that she could not simply

---

6. From the root *hyl*, NIV "to writhe in pain or anxiety"; BDB, 297.
7. "Instruct" in the NIV is too weak.

approach the king whenever she liked. Just like everyone else, she also had to be summoned by him. According to his law, if she went to the king she could be put to death, unless he held out his golden scepter. Esther said that this was public knowledge; "All the king's officials and the people of the royal provinces know [*yada*]," so Mordecai also would have known this. Thus, the main problem for Esther was that she had not been called to go to the king for 30 days (v. 11). Apparently, she previously had gone to the king unbidden to reveal to him the planned assassination attempt (2:22). That was when she was favored by the king. Now it seemed the king did not favor her any more. Given that he probably had a harem numbering 300 or more, most likely another woman or women would have been warming his bed in the meantime.

Remember that King Xerxes had chosen Esther out of all the women in his empire to be his queen. However, Esther hesitated now because she was not sure whether the king would extend his scepter towards her to accept her approach. Note that her reply to Mordecai did not refer to her social identity as a Jew. The personal aspect of her identity as the queen was more important to her. It would take much more effort for Mordecai to persuade her to act as a Jew.

When we reflect on Esther's response to Mordecai, we might be taken aback that she would defy her father-figure in this way. Her response was not even softened by any words that gave her father-figure respect or honor, which was the ideal in OT Law (e.g., Exod 20:12; Deut 5:16). Specifically, he was her cousin, but he had raised her as his own daughter from the time her parents had died (2:7). Even when she was brought into the palace, he did not fully relinquish his parental role, as we find him anxiously pacing about outside her room, waiting for morsels of information about how she was faring (2:11). She dutifully obeyed her guardian by keeping her Jewish identity secret (2:10, 20). However, now that she was asked to act on the basis of her Jewish identity, she was very reluctant, and from an Asian perspective, perhaps too strong in her response.

Yet, while not yet identifying with the social aspect of her identity, her forceful tone reflected the grave danger she must have been feeling as she considered approaching the king. For those who feel that Esther should have obeyed her guardian no matter what he commanded, we need to bear in mind that the fifth commandment enjoins the honoring of, not obedience to, parents. In the NT Paul reinforced the fifth commandment. He said that children were to obey their parents "in the Lord" and to honor their father and mother

(Eph 6:1–3).[8] Thus, the general principle still applies to us today, although how we honor our parents will vary depending on each individual situation.

4:12–17 SCENE 3: MORDECAI PERSUADED ESTHER

Mordecai was not so easily put off. Perhaps Esther thought, "I'm the queen so I'm safely tucked away in my quarters. Anyway, if I keep my Jewish identity secret I'll be safe from Haman's decree." However, when Esther's response was relayed to Mordecai (v. 12), he stopped her line of thinking immediately. He said, (1) If you keep quiet about your Jewish identity you still will not be safe (v. 13). Even though Esther lived in the palace, it ultimately would not protect her. (2) If you do not act on behalf of your people, they will still be rescued. Deliverance will come from "another place," but you will perish and your father's house with you (v. 14). That is the gist of his reply to her.

What he said specifically needs further discussion. The goal of "relief" (*revakh*; v. 14) for the Jews continues a motif found in the book of Esther. Haman suggested that it was not in the best interest of the king to give the Jews "relief" or "rest" (*nuakh*; 3:8). Yet the deliverance of the Jews will finally bring them "relief" or "rest" (*nuakh*; 9:16, 17, 18, 22).

There has been much discussion about the origin of this relief (v. 14). Mordecai said it would come from "another place" (*maqom aher*). Some suggest that this "place" is a veiled reference to God. In Deuteronomy "the place" (*hammaqom*) refers to God's dwelling place, Zion (e.g., Deut 12:5, 11, 14, 18, 21, 26). However, in Esther it is "another place" not "the place." A reference to Zion seems out of place in a narrative that does not mention the Promised Land or Zion elsewhere. Moreover, a contrast between deliverance by the hand of Esther ("place"?) and deliverance from God ("another place") does not make sense.[9] In the book of Esther, deliverance was from God only, either through Esther or someone else from "another place."[10] This understanding is reinforced if the fasting of Esther and the Jews reflected their dependence

---

8. Esther is a "young woman" of marriageable age, not a "child," so she does not need to obey her father-figure.
9. So David J. A. Clines, *Ezra, Nehemiah, Esther*, NCBC (Grand Rapids, MI: Eerdmans, 1984), 302.
10. The text does not state from where this deliverance would come. Suggestions include "outside the palace" and Greece; see Greg Goswell, "Keeping God Out of the Book of Esther," *EvQ* 82 (2010): 103; David G. Firth, *The Message of Esther: God Present but Unseen*, BST (Nottingham, UK: InterVarsity Press, 2010), 76.

upon and petition to God for deliverance – as we discussed above. It is also reinforced by our interpretation of "who knows?" below.

What is the meaning of Mordecai's subsequent statement, that if Esther did not take responsibility, deliverance would still come for the Jews, but she and her "father's house" (*beyth-av*) would perish (v. 14)? Her "father's house" would be roughly equivalent to her nuclear and extended family with her father as the head.[11] However, since Esther was an orphan, was this just an empty threat?[12] Or, since Esther did not seem to have any other living family members, did her father's house mean her and Mordecai? If so, why should Mordecai die if Esther remained silent?

Most likely, Mordecai was suggesting that she would be punished for not acting, and if she perished as the last member of her father's house, that would spell the end of her family line.[13] This interpretation finds support by comparison with the Greek manuscripts. In both the LXX and the AT, Mordecai's intimate relationship with Esther was central to his argument. He reminded her that he had raised her, and he pleaded with her to "speak to the king about *us*, and deliver *us* from death" (4:8, LXX; emphasis added). It seems the author(s) of MT Esther deliberately excluded reference to Mordecai's personal relationship with Esther. Based on this comparison, Mordecai would be included in Esther's father's house in the Greek manuscripts but not in the MT.

Previously Mordecai focused on her social identity as a Jew; now he focused on her family social identity. In Asia, often a person's "foremost identity is defined in relation to his or her family."[14] This includes extended family, as well as deceased ancestors. We can thus understand the gravity of the situation presented to Esther. Genealogies in the Bible reflect the importance of carrying on the family name and the family line. Esther did not want to be responsible for cutting off her family line.

---

11. The spheres of kinship relations in the OT are the father's house, clan, tribe and nation (e.g., Josh 7:16–18; Judg 6:15; 1 Sam 10:20–21). See Shunya Bendor, *The Social Structure of Ancient Israel: The Institution of the Family (beit 'ab) from the Settlement to the End of the Monarchy.* Jerusalem Biblical Studies 7 (Jerusalem, Israel: Simor, 1996). The patriarch of a father's house was normally the oldest living male.

12. E.g., Adele Berlin, *Esther* (Philadephia, PA: Jewish Publication Society, 2001), 49, who comments that "it is not a question of logic, but of rhetoric."

13. Ronald W. Pierce, "The Politics of Esther and Mordecai: Courage or Compromise?," *BBR* 2 (1992): 87, suggests that Mordecai would make sure that Esther was killed if she did not stand up for her people. Based on the presentation of Mordecai's character as benevolent and protective character so far in the narrative (2:7, 10, 11, 20), this seems unlikely.

14. Simon Chan, *Grassroots Asian Theology: Thinking the Faith from the Ground Up* (Downers Grove, IL: InterVarsity Press, 2014), 42–43.

The dilemma for Esther was thus one of loyalty and allegiance. Would she continue her primary allegiance to King Xerxes and the Persians or commit her allegiance to the Jews? If she maintained her allegiance to the king, the outcome would not be that the Jews would not be saved. The outcome would be that she would perish (*abad*, the *qal* form of the verb; 4:14), not under Haman's edict (3:13, where the *piel* infinitive of *abad* is used ["to destroy"], and 4:7, where Mordecai repeats the infinitive form from Haman's edict to Esther), but under God's judgment. Even as she decided to commit herself to God and his people, she knew "perishing" was a possible outcome (4:16; the *qal* form of *abad*).

If God were to judge her for not acting, what form might this judgment take? In a book where God acts in hidden ways, this probably alludes to Esther's eventual death because she did not identify herself as a member of God's people. This differentiation of God's people as a physical and spiritual entity is present throughout the OT but gains greater prominence in the time that Esther is set – the post-exilic period. Also, her perishing would have spelled the end not just of her, but of her father's house – Abihail's house. Nonetheless, the larger father's house to which Mordecai belonged would continue, because he had pledged his allegiance to God and his people (3:4; 4:1–3).

In short, Mordecai said, "You think your life is at risk if you go to the king? . . . Your life is at risk if you do not." Faced with this cold hard reality, Esther really had no choice, did she? Mordecai concluded his argument by asking Esther to reflect on her life: "And who knows (*mi yada*) but that you have come to your royal position for such a time as this?" (v. 14). In the Wisdom Literature, the phrase "who knows?" often has a sense of uncertainty or of something not able to be known (e.g., Prov 24:22; Eccl 2:19; 3:21). However, elsewhere in the OT the phrase is used in the context of hope in God's providence in a time of crisis, usually God's judgment (2 Sam 12:22; Joel 2:14; Jonah 3:9).[15] This latter nuance better fits the context of Mordecai's sentence, "And who knows but that you have come to your royal position for such a time as this?"

---

15. Karen H. Jobes, *Esther,* NIVAC (Grand Rapids, MI: Zondervan, 1999), 135–137, finds other intertextual links between Esther 4 and Joel 2 in addition to *mi yada.* (1) The Hebrew phrase translated as "with fasting, weeping and wailing" occurs both in Joel 2:12 and Esth 4:3. (2) "Rend your heart and not your garments" (Joel 2:13) is similar to Mordecai's response to the decree. These inner-biblical allusions strengthen my reading of Esth 4:14.

Earlier in the verse, Mordecai said "this time," but now he says, "a time like this."[16] It was the suitable time for Esther to act, the perfect moment. Yet it was not a unique opportunity; many "times" like this will present themselves. In effect, Mordecai said, "Think about it, Esther: you were an orphaned Jewish girl plucked from obscurity to be queen. Could it be that you have been put in this place of influence for such a time as this? Could a hidden hand be behind your royal position for this exact moment?"

Esther then instructed all the Jews to fast for her along with her attendants, and after that preparation, she would go to the king (v. 16). Fasts in the Bible were usually during the day, until evening (e.g., Judg 20:26; 2 Sam 1:12). Today, our Muslim neighbors and friends fast during daylight hours in the Ramadan season. Here Esther called for the Jews to fast both day and night for three days. This showed her level of earnestness and how seriously she viewed her situation. Moreover, the fasting revealed her humility as she called on her community to fast along with her in order to seek God's favor.

She would then take the risk of going to the king, even though it was against the law. She had been loyal to the king and his decrees and laws up until then. Now that she faced a dilemma, she chose to identify with her people because too much was at stake. This would involve her acting not "according to the law," which reminds us of the actions of Daniel, Shadrach, Meshach, and Abednego (Dan 3:8–18). They refused to obey the law of the king when it went against that of God. Esther acted in the same vein in order to stave off the annihilation of her people.

Some commentators hear a note of "resignation to fate" in Esther's next statement: "And if I perish, I perish" (v. 16).[17] Yet coming straight after her instruction to fast (to seek God's favor), it is better to hear a note of "courageous determination" in her voice.[18] Perhaps it is similar to the Filipino phrase, "*bahala na*," which means something like, "let it be." "*Bahala*" is derived from an old Tagalog name for God – *Bathala*. So it's like saying, "God will take care of it."[19] This is similar to the sentiment of Daniel's friends as they faced

---

16. The noun *'eth* ("time") has two basic meanings: (1) "time of an event" and (2) "time for an event" (BDB, 773). The latter has four subcategories: (a) "usual time," (b) "the proper or suitable time," (c) "the appointed time," and (d) "uncertain time." Mordecai moved from "time of an event" (1) to "the proper or even appointed time for an event" (2b or c). He moved from quantity to quality, from a measurable moment to an opportune moment.

17. So, e.g., Leslie C. Allen and Timothy S. Laniak, *Ezra, Nehemiah, Esther* (Peabody, MA: Hendrickson, 2003), 228.

18. Clines, *Ezra, Nehemiah, Esther*, 303.

19. My thanks to Federico Villanueva for this cultural insight.

annihilation: "If we are thrown into the blazing furnace, the God we serve is able to deliver us from it, and he will deliver us from Your Majesty's hand. But even if he does not, we want you to know, Your Majesty, that we will not serve your gods or worship the image of gold you have set up" (Dan 3:17–18). Just like Daniel's friends, Esther was not sure if she would survive. She took the initiative to act, but she knew that she could not control the outcome. Yet she did all she could to prepare for her meeting with the king, and she drew others in to stand in solidarity with her, pleading to God, acknowledging that he was the one who could control the outcome.

Just like Mordecai and Esther, at times we need to act with initiative for the sake of God and his people. God can fulfil his purposes without us. However, he often chooses to use us. It is not that he needs us or his plans will go out the window. It is not that he only intervenes in the affairs of the world when things go wrong. His hidden hand even works in the everyday events of our lives. So as we face suffering for the sake of being Christians, we should pray like our lives depend on it. We should ask for others to pray along with us and perhaps also to fast for us. Then we can act with courage and initiative.

James Hudson Taylor was a missionary to China and the founder of the China Inland Mission (CIM). He was known as a man of prayer. The following quote is ascribed to him:

> In Shansi I found Chinese Christians who were accustomed to spend time in fasting and prayer. They recognized that this fasting, which so many dislike, which requires faith in God, since it makes one feel weak and poorly, is really a divinely-appointed means of grace. Perhaps the greatest hindrance to our work is our own imagined strength; and in fasting we learn what poor, weak creatures we are – dependent on a meal of meat for the little strength which we are so apt to lean upon.[20]

As Hudson Taylor depended upon God in prayer and fasting, he also attempted great things for God. His first visit to China was on September 19, 1853, and he ended up spending fifty-one years there.[21] CIM became OMF International, which celebrated its 150th anniversary in 2015. Today,

---

20. From http://christian-quotes.ochristian.com/Hudson-Taylor-Quotes/page-2.shtml (accessed December 6, 2017).
21. For more details, see Roger Steer, *J. Hudson Taylor: A Man in Christ* (Milton Keynes, UK: Authentic Publishing, 2001).

it has 1,400 workers from forty nations, serving approximately one hundred people groups.[22]

Esther 4 ends with a role reversal. Previously Mordecai gave commands for Esther to follow (2:10, 20; 4:8); now she "commanded" him (*tsavah*; 4:17). His task of persuading Esther completed, he now "moved on" (*abar*) to follow Esther's orders. Previously, Mordecai transgressed (participle form of *abar*) the king's command (*tsavah*) by not bowing to Haman (3:3); now he obeyed Esther's command by "moving on." Esther, who had come to the "royal position," was now ready to act with the power of a queen. However, more importantly, she was ready to identify with and act on behalf of her people.

Here, then, we have reached a turning point and not just in Esther's character. If we take the motif of "feasting" as guiding the structure of the book of Esther, then this chapter is a turning point for the storyline of the book. Four feasts precede this fast of Esther, Mordecai and the Jews (1:1–4, 5–8, 9; 2:18), and four feasts follow it (5:1–8; 7:1–10; 8:15–17; 9:16–10:3).[23]

22. For a video of OMF International's history, see https://omf.org/about-omf/ (accessed December 6, 2017).
23. See Pierce, "Politics," 79. While this is *a* turning point, the major turning point will be in chapter 6.

IDENTIFY YOURSELF

Like Esther, the Jews in the Persian Empire might have been tempted to become just like everyone else. Follow the Persian customs, follow the Persian law, and even follow the Persian religion. Perhaps some of them *were* God's people in name only. Their primary loyalty and allegiance might have been to the Persian Empire.

I would suggest that this is one reason why God was not mentioned in the Esther narrative. God's name was deliberately withheld from the narrative so that Jewish readers would fill in where God should be. God's people fill in where they should have fasted *and prayed*. God's people fill in where Mordecai should have said that deliverance would come *from God*. By not mentioning God, the narrative uses a kind of "reverse psychology" to fire up patriotism and loyalty in the hearts of God's people. In particular, not mentioning God spurs the readers, and us, to identify as God's people even if it might bring us suffering – or death.

The way Esther was described also induces the reader to identify with God's people. Mordecai was "Mordecai the Jew" but Esther was neither "Esther the Jew" nor "Esther the Persian," even after she was the queen. Mordecai only had a Persian name, but Esther also had a Jewish name – Hadassah (2:7). Esther's Jewish ancestry, her father Abihail, was mentioned at the beginning and end of the narrative (2:15; 9:29). Thus, although Esther could change her primary allegiance, the narrative hints that Esther's ethnicity was always Jewish. Those who live in a multi-ethnic society must likewise choose to identify with God's people.[1]

Hilmy Nor was willing to identify as a Christian despite the consequences. He was born into a Malay Muslim family and then became a Christian while working at a multi-national oil company. His Christian witness led to his being overlooked for a promotion and the lobbying by Muslims at his workplace to have his position terminated. He was detained in jail under the Internal Security Act of Malaysia for 14 months, including two months in solitary confinement. He was separated from his wife, and he lost 35 pounds. Yet he was able to write this: "[My wife and I] had the privilege of 'representing' [God] and [we] feel blessed to be used by Him."[2]

Identifying as a Christian may be costly. This choice may have consequences for ourselves, our loved ones, or even for a whole people group (as in the case of Esther). We often do not know how God will use our decisions or what the outcomes will be for us. Today, as a church, we may be tempted to keep silent instead of raising our voices for Christ. Each of us might want to keep silent instead of speaking up for Christ at work or school, among friends or family, or before the authorities.

We need to remember that we do not belong to the world; we belong to Christ (John 15:19). Jesus says that it is costly to identify with him, and we need to count that cost as we follow him (Luke 14:25–33). Yet, like Esther, we can act in faith with courage and determination. Who knows if God has arranged our circumstances for such a time as this?

---

1. For a diasporic reading of the book of Esther by an Asian American from Malaysia, see Jeffrey Kah-Jin Kuan, "Diasporic Reading of a Diasporic Text: Identity Politics and Race Relations and the Book of Esther," in *Interpreting Beyond Borders*, ed. Fernando F. Segovia (Sheffield, UK: Sheffield Academic Press, 2000), 161–173.
2. Hilmy Nor, *Circumcised Heart* (Petaling Jaya, Malaysia: Kairos Research Centre, 1999), 6.

ESTHER 5

Everybody makes plans, some for the near future and some far in advance. We plan what we will do in the next hour or next week. Some of us make plans for the next year or the next decade. Others of us might even plan for our retirement. Indeed, many governments in Asia push us to think about our lives in retirement, especially as we need to contribute to superannuation or provident funds. Of course we all need to make some plans for our lives, either for the day ahead or the far horizon of our retirement. However, as we do so, we need to remember that our plans are always tentative because we all live our lives within God's greater overall plan.

The last chapter ended with Esther finally accepting the challenge to identify with the Jews and help them in their predicament. With determination she formulated a plan and started to put it into action as she called for a communal fast. Her plan seems to derive from her own initiative, as there is no mention of her receiving advice from anyone – not Mordecai, not Hegai, and not Hathach.

In this chapter of Esther, we find two of the main characters making plans. Esther revealed more of her plan in the first scene (vv. 1–8); then Haman made his plans in the second (vv. 9–14). So far in the book of Esther, we have seen how banquets were occasions where important events occurred. Will another important event unfold at the banquet Esther has planned?

5:1–8 SCENE 1: ESTHER APPROACHED THE KING

At the end of the three days of fasting, Esther prepared to approach the king (v. 1). In contrast to Vashti who refused to wear her royal crown before the king (1:10–12), Esther dressed up in her full royal attire. She knew her external appearance would be crucial as she made an unbidden appearance before King Xerxes. From first-hand experience, she knew that he had a soft spot for attractive women. However, she also knew the importance of "power dressing."[1] In some Western cultures, informal clothing is worn by people from different levels of society. In Asia, however, we understand the significance of dressing up: uniforms indicate rank; formal attire is important to express and gain respect; religious garb is required for ceremonies. Literally, Esther put on "royalty" (*malkuth*), which primarily refers to her royal robes, but also alludes

---

1. Kandy Queen-Sutherland, *Ruth and Esther* (Macon, GA: Smyth & Helwys, 2016), 310.

to the authority of her position. Elsewhere in the OT, people were clothed in concepts like "righteousness" (Ps 132:9) or "salvation" (Isa 6:10). In the previous chapter, Mordecai stated that Esther had attained "royal position (*malkuth*) for such a time as this" (4:14). She now dressed for the part.

As she approached the king, we wonder if he will let her in to see him or not. We know her life is at risk (4:11). The word for "king" (*mlk*) is used six times in verse 1 to highlight the challenge facing Esther. In the MT, there is no mention of her facial expression, but the Greek Additions describe her as "radiant with perfect beauty, and she looked happy."[2] Some people may view her entrance to the inner court without prior request as an act of disobedience. Yet we can read 5:1–2 as consistent with her *attitude* of obedience: she stayed in the inner court and only entered the throne upon the king's invitation.[3] If she did break a Persian decree (4:11), it is a little surprising that the king did not raise this as an issue or mention any punishment.[4]

In any case, Esther cleverly placed herself in the inner court but in line of sight of the king, who was in the throne room. As soon as Xerxes spotted her, he invited her into his presence. She immediately won favor or grace (*nasa hen*) in his sight, as she had won his "favor and approval" (*nasa hen wahesed*) by winning the contest (2:17), as well as "the favor of everyone who saw her" (2:15). The king quickly extended his scepter, and she touched its tip, probably to recognize the king's authority and to accept his grace (v. 2). She was saved from the death penalty, and so we can let out a sigh of relief. So we wonder: Was Esther over-playing the risk of approaching the king? Or were her concerns a reflection of her sensitivity to her husband's lack of desire for her at the time (4:11)?

In any case, she has his goodwill now. He made a grand offer to her: "What is it, Queen Esther? What is your request? Even up to half the kingdom, it will be given you" (v. 3). This sounds like a generous offer, and it was. Indeed, it is consistent with what we have seen of the king in chapters 1–2: extravagant and

---

2. Addition D:5 (LXX). This would have been no mean feat since she had fasted for the previous three days. The Addition also colorfully describes her inner state: "Her heart was frozen with fear."

3. Jon D. Levenson, *Esther*, OTL (Louisville, KY: Westminster John Knox, 1997), 89. David J. A. Clines, *Ezra, Nehemiah, Esther*, NCBC (Grand Rapids, MI: Eerdmans, 1984), 304, comments that it "must be a day of audience, for otherwise the entrance would not be open." Perhaps Esther knew that on that day he would be more accessible, even without prior request.

4. Certainly, Esther took a risk by approaching the king, but based on King Ahasuerus not killing Vashti for her "insubordination," Esther should have known that it would have been unlikely that King Ahasuerus would kill her for visiting him uninvited. See Ronald W. Pierce, "The Politics of Esther and Mordecai: Courage or Compromise?," *BBR* 2 (1992): 87.

excessive. King Xerxes was probably not speaking literally when he offered up to half his kingdom. Although, according to the Greek historian Herodotus, Xerxes made at least one other similarly generous offer.

> [Xerxes] asked [Artaynte] what she wanted in return for her favors, for he would deny nothing at her asking . . . . She said to Xerxes, 'Will you give me whatever I ask of you?' He promised this, supposing that she would ask anything . . . . He accordingly offered her cities instead and gold in abundance and an army for none but herself to command.[5]

Furthermore, in the NT, Herod made a similar offer to Herodias's daughter: "Whatever you ask I will give you, up to half my kingdom" (Mark 6:23).[6] So the king was probably saying something like, "What do you want Esther? Ask for whatever you want." The equivalent today would be handing someone a blank check. The temptation would have been for Esther to make the request at that time. If we were in Esther's place, perhaps some of us would have made our request then and there. However, Esther did not make her request. She had something else in mind first. She invited the king and Haman to come to a banquet that she had prepared (v. 4).

So the king summoned his prime minister, and they went to Esther's banquet (v. 5). As they enjoyed their wine after the main meal, the king again asked her to present her request. By responding to the king's question using his same words ("petition" and "request"), it seems as if she was giving her answer. She drew out her response with two phrases indicating submission and respect ("if the king regards me with favor," "if it pleases the king"). By saying that it was *her* petition and request, she made this answer sound personal. Thus, she did not reveal that her petition actually affected other people – until later when she revealed her true request. In the end, Esther delayed until the day after to "do as the king has said" (vv. 7–8; ESV).

We are not told why she delayed her request. In Asia, we might sense that it was not the social custom to make the request so soon. Or, we might sense that she knew that the way to a man's heart was through his stomach – so with another round of food and wine, the king will be more likely to say, "Yes!" Perhaps she just sensed that it was not the right time to ask. Whatever

---

5. Herodotus 9.109.2–3.
6. In both these episodes, the kings (Xerxes and Herod) made open-ended offers to women that they ended up regretting.

the reason, Esther kept the king in suspense – and us in suspense as well.[7] At the very least, Esther was wise to ask for Haman to be present before she presented her request. She needed to catch Haman off guard as she presented her request to the king, otherwise he might have been able to wriggle his way out of his situation. However, since the king had not been able to make decisions by himself in the narrative so far, Esther needed to present her request in a way that prompted "the king to immediate action."[8] As readers of the Esther narrative, we just hope she knows what she is doing.

Elsewhere in the OT, we find other women making crucial interventions.[9] Abigail successfully pleaded with David not to shed Nabal's blood (1 Sam 25:24–35). In a parable, the woman of Tekoa pled with King David to save the life of her son, because his death would have meant the end of her husband's family line (2 Sam 14:4–17). The son turned out to actually be David's son, Absalom. Intriguingly, Esther was making an intervention that would save many more lives, but her approach was much more indirect.

Overall, in approaching the king with her request, Esther seems to be following a careful plan. A plan that seems to come from her initiative alone.[10] She dressed up in a way that was befitting of a queen (v. 1), she placed herself in the right position to be noticed by the king (vv. 1–2), and she spoke with a submissive tone (vv. 4, 7–8). When she was asked to make her request, her delay seemed to be part of her plan and not a sign of indecision or fear.

Yet plan as she may, we know from the Bible that in the end, everything that takes place in the world is under God's control. As it says in Proverbs 16:9, "In their hearts humans plan their course, but the LORD establishes their steps." Further, Jesus said that not even a sparrow falls to the ground without

---

7. Linda M. Day, *Esther*, Abingdon Old Testament Commentaries (Nashville, TN: Abingdon Press, 2005), 99–100, lists some of the possibilities: she wanted Xerxes more inebriated; she wanted the king to become accustomed to her presence again; she wanted to heighten his curiosity; she needed to build up her courage; she played the role of hostess so that she was not so threatening to Xerxes; as the king repeated his promises, she wanted him to feel even more committed to fulfilling those promises; she wanted Haman to feel unthreatened, to surprise him; another party would further please Xerxes. Those who adopt a close reading of the text argue that Esther delayed in order to maneuver the king "into committing himself in advance"; e.g., Frederic W. Bush, *Ruth, Esther*, WBC 9 (Dallas, TX: Word Books, 1996), 407. This is hard to discern through a normal reading of the text, and it is questionable whether the original hearers would have detected this. Moreover, the king had already committed himself to carrying out Esther's request (5:3, 6).

8. Bush, *Ruth, Esther*, 407.

9. Levenson, *Esther*, 90.

10. The narrative does not mention that she received advice from anyone about approaching the king, including Mordecai or Hegai.

God knowing (Matt 10:29). Esther followed her plan, but only God knew if she would be successful. Also consider the teaching of James, the brother of Jesus (Jas 4:13–15). In our lives, we do not know what will happen tomorrow. Indeed, it is sobering to be reminded that our lives are like mists that linger for a while and then vanish. Thus, we cannot make definite plans for our lives. Most of us in Asia often hear about the idea of "fate" in other religions. For instance, our Muslim neighbors might speak of *qadar*, the idea of divine destiny. More likely, we will hear them say, "*Insha'Allah*," which means "if God wills." As James teaches us, we can put our trust in the one who controls our future. We express our trust by saying, "If it is the Lord's will," we will live and do this or that (Jas 4:15).

5:9–14 SCENE 2: HAMAN'S INVITATION SPOILED

Haman left the banquet elated and perhaps a bit drunk ("happy and in high spirits" v. 9). "High spirits" (*tov lev*) was also the description of King Xerxes' mood just before he commanded Queen Vashti to his banquet earlier in the book (1:10). Haman was like Xerxes, so we wonder if he was about to do something ill-judged that would bring his happiness to an end. If he had too much wine, we can expect that he would be disinhibited. This is what we find when he saw Mordecai at the king's gate. There Mordecai refused to show Haman any form of public honor (he did not rise or show "fear" on account of Haman). He did not give "face." Previously Mordecai refused to bow (3:2), and now in this passage, he refused to stand or even stir (*zu'a*; NIV show "fear"; ESV "tremble"). Haman (*haman*) was filled with rage (*hemah*). His mood swung violently from exultant to furious. Yet he managed to restrain himself; perhaps he knew that there was not much he could do for the moment. This lack of respect was what had triggered his edict in the first place (3:1–6), so perhaps Haman thought he would get his revenge when his edict was enacted.

Then Haman called his wife, Zeresh, and his friends to come to his house (v. 10). Next, he did something on which we generally look down in Malaysia. He began to brag in front of his friends and his wife. Previously he was full of rage; now he was full of himself. He boasted about four things: the glory of his riches, his many sons, his honor from the king, and his promotion above the other nobles and officials (v. 11). In the OT, wealth and children (especially sons) were signs of success (Job 1:2–3; 42:10–15). Yet surely his wife and friends must have already known of his achievements and possessions.

We all know people like Haman. We invite them to share tea or coffee, and the whole time they just talk about themselves. We can understand Haman's seeking reassurance from his close friends and family. We can empathize with someone who has had a bad day at work. We can even accept someone who is confident. However, when over-confidence becomes arrogance, then that person is hard to tolerate. It is thus likely that his boasting was frowned upon by the original audience of the Esther narrative.

Moreover, Haman continued this self-promotion by saying that he had just dined with the king and his wife and that he had been invited to another special exclusive meal. No one else received an invitation to the private banquet, only him (v. 12). "I'm part of the king's inner circle," he thought. Yet his line of thinking soon followed the same route as his path home from the palace: it swung from joyful to downcast. "But all this gives me no satisfaction as long as I see that Jew Mordecai sitting at the king's gate" (v. 13). He may have received honor for his achievements, especially from the king, but he received none from Mordecai. Haman complained that he would not be able to enjoy his anticipated intimate meal with Xerxes and Esther because Mordecai the Jew remained a thorn in his side (vv. 9, 13).

His close circle then made a suggestion: "Why not do away with him?" They advised him to build a 50 cubit (22.5 m; about six stories) high pole. If this height is taken literally, it would be higher than any building in Susa.[11] His close circle advised Haman to ask the king to impale this pesky Jew on it the next morning, before Esther's next feast (v. 14).[12] Just as the proposal of King Xerxes' advisor pleased the king, so the proposal of Haman's advisors pleased Haman (1:21; 5:14).

Yet we might feel a little uncomfortable with this proposal. Elsewhere in the Esther narrative, commands were issued by higher-status people to lower-status people (4:16 [2x]; 5:5; 6:10 [3x]; 7:9; 8:8 [2x]). Here Zeresh and Haman's friends used an imperative (strong command) instead of a jussive (mild command or strong wish) for "said" (*'emor*). Moreover, was this proposal skirting on the edge of, if not beyond, the bounds of the Persian governmental/administrative system? It seems Haman would "say to" (*'emor*; ESV "tell")

---

11. The palace in Susa was estimated to be 40 to 50 feet high (12 to 15 meters); Adele Berlin, *Esther* (Philadephia, PA: Jewish Publication Society, 2001), 55.

12. Karen H. Jobes, *Esther*, NIVAC (Grand Rapids, MI: Zondervan, 1999), 145, draws a comparison between Zeresh's advice to Haman, and Jezebel's to King Ahab (1 Kgs 21:1–16). Ahab's power and entitlements failed to satisfy him because he wanted Naboth's vineyard. Jezebel's advice was to do away with Naboth.

instead of "ask" (NIV, NJPS) the king to hang Mordecai (v. 14). We bridle at the presumption. Esther carefully worked within the system; Haman bent it to his desires. Furthermore, with a hint of irony, Haman took advice from "Zeresh, his wife, along with all his friends." Zeresh's position in the phrase gives her prominence, although his friends also agreed to the proposal. Of course, wise husbands are open to advice from their wives. However, we see here that something is not quite right about who had the power in Haman's household – especially in light of the king's earlier edict for husbands to take control of their households (1:22).

Like King Xerxes, Haman was open to questionable advice. "A perfect solution," thought Haman, as he gleefully ordered that the pole be built. Haman could not wait eleven months to destroy Mordecai: he wanted to kill him now! The patience of Esther and the petulance of Haman were thus contrasted. The exaggerated height of the pole would heighten Mordecai's public shaming, as it would be seen from a greater distance. Yet, the pole's height was really appropriate for a man like Haman: an oversized pole for an oversized ego.

That was clearly one of Haman's major character flaws: above all, he sought the honor of men. He talked about his possessions and achievements because he wanted to be admired for them. We mentioned before that the lack of job security was part of the Persian system, which may have contributed to his personal insecurity. Yet we do not find that same sense of insecurity and grasping for honor in either Esther or Mordecai.[13] Esther won the king's favor, but she waited for the honor to be granted to her. Similarly, for Mordecai, honor would be given to him as a gift from the king (6:11; 8:1–2). Esther and Mordecai both gained honor, but it was not the driving force of their lives. For Haman, externals were his source of honor and pride. Thus, our alarm bells should ring as we recall two proverbs: (1) "The LORD detests all the proud of heart. Be sure of this: They will not go unpunished" (Prov 16:5). (2) "Pride goes before destruction, a haughty spirit before a fall" (Prov 16:18). Haman was a proverbial fool. Dark clouds were on his horizon.

When we reflect on our lives, we might find that we are sometimes like Haman. We are tempted to place pride in our possessions and achievements. We are tempted to seek honor from those around us. Since bragging is frowned upon in many Asian cultures, we may brag in an indirect manner. A pastor may share about how many churches he has planted. A church member may talk

---

13. Esther was understandably unsure about the king's favor (4:11), and Mordecai did not complain about his lack of recognition after saving the king (2:19–23).

about her donations for children living in slums. This kind of sharing may spur us on to love and good deeds, or we may squirm at the sense of self-promotion from the person. When sharing publicly, it is sometimes difficult to deflect the glory back to God. Perhaps we can also share about our weaknesses and God's grace in strengthening us (2 Cor 11–12). For God's opposition to the proud is repeated in the NT (e.g., Jas 4:6; 1 Pet 5:5). According to the Apostle Paul, the only true basis for our boasting is "in the Lord" Jesus Christ (1 Cor 1:28–31).

So as the chapter ends, we see that both Esther and Haman have laid plans. Esther's table was set for feasting. Haman's pole was erected for lynching. However, within God's plan, whose plan would be successful?

ESTHER AND POLITICS

Power, especially political power, is a major theme in the book of Esther. There was jostling for position and influence in the Persian court and the king's harem. Haman gained power but did not receive the honor that he thought was due to him (3:5; 5:9). Esther gained the position that she sought above other contenders. Mordecai's refusal to acknowledge Haman's position led to a direct clash with Esther, whom Mordecai convinced to use her power to ensure the survival of the Jewish people.[1] In this chapter, Esther put on her royal robes and the power that came with them (5:1).

The book of Esther does not mention God and indeed leaves out any religious references. Yet it is highly likely that the first Jewish readers would have discerned God's working in the narrative. Reading Esther within the context of the whole Bible, especially keeping in mind God's promises to his people and his purposes for them, would reinforce this understanding. Elsewhere in the Old Testament, God's people were thrust into positions of authority in foreign courts. A major difference is that God's presence and influence in events is directly stated. He is described as working in Egypt, in the lives of Joseph and Moses. He is described as controlling events in the place of power in Babylon and Persia, where Daniel and his friends serve. Yet in the Esther narrative God did not speak to Esther or Mordecai. He did not appear to them in a burning bush. He did not appear to them in dreams. He is not said to control or influence the foreigners who are in power, King Xerxes and Haman.

This ordinary flavor of the Esther narrative makes it particularly applicable to politics in Asia today. In some countries, like Malaysia, faith is drawn into political discussions for religious, social, or often political reasons. In other Asian countries, faith is not. Yet within any of these contexts, how can Christians work in the political sphere when God does not give specific instructions? The book of Esther is instructive in at least four ways.

First, it is possible to be a member of a minority group and still work within the prevalent socio-political structure. Mordecai and Esther were Jews who served the Persian Empire. Haman was also a foreigner but did not always follow protocol (5:14). Christian politicians in Asia today might be members of a minority group, but they can still remain loyal to the government and promote its interests.

Second, working with a government does not mean having to agree with all its decisions. Mordecai and Esther did not agree with Haman's edict. Yet they were able to change a decision of the king by working within the Persian legal framework. Esther did not seek to incite her people to rebel against the state. Christians who are in government (either as government servants or in a position of power) should work wisely to bring about change for the common good.

Third, Christian politicians can act responsibly, knowing that God can use their actions within his plan and purposes. Without God's direct instructions, politicians will need to make decisions without certainty about the outcome. Mordecai still trusted that God would act in some way to deliver his people (4:14). Esther took the initiative to act without knowing whether she would be successful but entrusting the outcome to God (4:16). Just like in the rest of life, we might only see God at work in political decisions as we look back.

Fourth, Christians in positions of power can ask others to stand in solidarity with them before God. Esther asked all the Jews to fast with her (4:16). Today, Christian politicians can do likewise, as well as ask for prayer. In the latter, they would have the support of the Apostle Paul, who enjoins Christians to pray for kings and all who are in authority (1 Tim 2:1–2) – Christian and non-Christian alike.

These four insights assume that a politician works within the prevalent socio-political structure. This is how God worked in the stories of Esther and Daniel, as well as in other parts of the OT. However, as Richard Bauckham points out, "In the teaching of Jesus . . . we find a radical critique of the kind of power the Gentiles exercised, requiring not a mere reversal of the power-situation but a reversal of values (Mark 10:42–44)."[2] Jesus' vision was one of serving rather than lording power over others – just as he demonstrated in his life. Whether we, in Asia, are politicians or not, may we use the power God has given us to serve others, as we look forward to the day when we will reign with him, the risen servant King (2 Tim 2:12).

---

1. For a political reading of the book of Esther from a Jewish perspective, see Yoram Hazony, *God and Politics in Esther*, 2nd ed. (Cambridge, UK: Cambridge University Press, 2016).
2. Richard Bauckham, *The Bible in Politics: How to Read the Bible Politically*, 2nd ed. (London, UK: SPCK, 2010), 128.

ESTHER 6

There is a Chinese proverb: *fēng huí lù zhuǎn*[1] (the mountain road twists and turns). This proverb is based on the observation that although a mountain track may be difficult or even hazardous, you never know when you will reach a turn in your journey where the path suddenly becomes smooth and easy. A similar idiom in English is "to take a turn," either for the better or for the worse. The Chinese proverb has more of a positive sense, figuratively speaking of the coming of an unexpected opportunity. The English idiom can be used for a turning point leading to either an improving or worsening condition.

Esther 6 contains the major turning point in the narrative. Things have been building up to this point in the story, and here is the turning point where fortunes start to turn, in particular for Haman and Mordecai. At the end of chapter 5, Mordecai was under a death sentence. In this chapter, things are now about to change for him and the Jewish people. Haman had been promoted to second-in-command in the Persian Empire, but here he began to fall. In this chapter things turn for the worse for Haman, but turn for the better for Mordecai.

The Chinese proverb gives no hint of any power causing the turnaround. People just continue on their journeys in life and things just happen to change. However, there are hints in this chapter that the reversals are not just nature taking its course. The many coincidences and the chance events point to a powerful hand working behind what can be seen. The tensions in the Esther narrative are not all solved by the end of this chapter, but the story reveals that God is directing the path to their resolution.

The chapter opens with the king not able to sleep (vv. 1–5). This led to a series of unlikely events, ending with Haman having to honor Mordecai (vv. 6–11). Haman's fall had begun (vv. 12–14).

6:1–5 SCENE 1: THE SLEEP OF THE KING FLED

Our attention now turns to King Xerxes, who was in his palace. It just so happened that he could not fall asleep that night (literally, "the sleep of the king fled [*nadad*]"; NIV "the king could not sleep"). The ruler of the vast Persian Empire must have had many things on his mind. Uprisings and assassination plots were real threats for a king in ancient West Asia. Perhaps contributing

---

1. 峰回路转.

to his insomnia this night were thoughts about the possible things his queen might request from him. After all, she had already left him in suspense twice.

What do we do when we cannot sleep? We might watch a slow movie, we might drink some warm milk, or we might settle down with a comforting book. How did the king try to fall asleep? The last option: he ordered that the historical chronicles of his reign be brought and read to him (v. 1). These are probably the same records as mentioned in 2:23 (see also Ezra 5:17). The king probably hoped that the monotonous sound of the reader's voice, along with the boring subject matter would send him to sleep. However, the king's readers just happened to choose a certain volume of the chronicles. That volume just happened to fall open at the page which described Mordecai saving the king's life by exposing the conspirators Bigthan and Teresh (2:19–23). That event also apparently just happened, but now that it came to light it was about to take on a greater importance.

So now the king was not feeling sleepy; in fact, his eyes were wide open. "What honor and distinction has Mordecai received for this?" asked the king. "Nothing has been done for him," replied the king's attendants (v. 3).

The king realized that not honoring Mordecai was a serious oversight that he needed to correct. Not only must a reputable and judicious king punish those who do wrong (like Bigthan and Teresh), he also must publicly honor those who deserve it – especially those who have shown their loyalty to the king by saving his life. Herodotus lists two such instances. In one instance King Xerxes granted land to two captains, as well as being recorded as "the king's benefactors."[2] In the other instance Xerxes installed a man as ruler of Cilicia for saving the life of the king's brother.[3] However, in the Esther narrative no reward for Mordecai had been recorded in the chronicles of King Xerxes' reign.

So far in the narrative, the king had only acted based on advice from his counsellors. He was now faced with the problem of working out how to honor Mordecai. When he said, "Who is in the court?" (v. 4), he may have been asking for who might be around to offer advice. Or it may have been that he heard someone come into the court, or that he spied the person from the corner of his eye. Whatever the reason, who happened to arrive? The king's closest advisor! But why was Haman entering the king's court so early? Because he could not wait to have Mordecai impaled on the pole he had prepared for him (v. 4). Haman had come to "speak to" (*'amar*) the king about Mordecai,

---

2. Herodotus 8.85.
3. Herodotus 9.107.

not "ask" him (5:14). His advisors told him to go "in the morning," but he was so eager he came very early in the morning – apparently before dawn. The king's attendants seemed surprised to see the prime minister, as they say, "Look (*hinneh*)! Haman is standing in the court." So the king invited him inside (v. 5).

Let us just pause the narrative for a moment to reflect on this scene. It just so happened that the king could not sleep that night. It just so happened that Xerxes found out that Mordecai had not been rewarded – at the very same time that Haman was about to ask the king to hang Mordecai. Do you think these were just coincidences?

One way that God's actions are presented in the book of Esther is through these "chance happenings." From our viewpoint, we are surprised that things can just fall into place so easily. During the Second World War, Yap Chwee Lan rescued many from her town, Kampung Baru, Johor, in Malaysia, because she could speak Japanese. Her father died when she was seven years old, so she had to work to support her family. At age thirteen she had worked with a Japanese hairdresser and learned the Japanese language. Two years later the Japanese Occupation began. She was able to save people in her town because she was able to vouch for them as not belonging to the resistance – in Japanese.[4] When we reflect on Yap Chwee Lan's life, it might seem things just so happened.

Things just seem to happen in the Esther narrative also. However, do not be fooled: there are too many "coincidences" for these to be just luck or chance. Again, it was the hidden hand of God working behind the scenes. In the NT, the Apostle Paul told the Athenians,

> From one man he made all the nations, that they should inhabit the whole earth; and he marked out their appointed times in history and the boundaries of their lands. God did this so that they would seek him and perhaps reach out for him and find him, though he is not far from any one of us. (Acts 17:26–27)

God guides all people in all places in the world so that we might seek him. As we look back on our lives, we can see how God arranged people and events so that we sought him. As we look back at how God saved us, we too can identify a chain of events that seemed to just fall into place.

---

4. Vivienne Wong, *Grandma in JB Saved Countless Lives during World War II Because She Could Speak Japanese*, April 7, 2017, available from http://www.asiaone.com/malaysia/grandma-jb-saved-countless-lives-during-world-war-ii-because-she-could-speak-japanese (accessed December 12, 2017).

6:6–11 SCENE 2: HAMAN HONORED MORDECAI

Haman entered the court. However, before he could say a word the king asked Haman, "What should be done for the man the king delights to honor?" (v. 6). Such an indirect question would not be unusual in a king's court. We find it elsewhere in the OT (2 Sam 12:1–12; 14:1–24). Yet the indirectness was not the only difference between the way Xerxes phrased the question to Haman and the way he had phrased it to his attendants.[5] To his attendants he mentioned "honor" (*yekar*) and "promotion" (*gedulah*), along with Mordecai's name. To Haman he only mentioned "honor." Since Haman had already received "promotion" (*giddal*; 3:1) and only heard "honor," he was more inclined to think he was the one to receive the honor. Nonetheless, the next part of the verse gives us a special insight into the mind of Haman.[6] Haman immediately thought the king wanted to honor him. "Who else could it be?" he thought (v. 6). He was so egotistical that he could not imagine the honor was for anyone else. Haman had come to make an execution request, but his pride and lust for honor distracted him and pointed him in another direction altogether. The king's question might have thrown him off balance, but it was the size of his head that toppled him.

His eagerness to be feted was revealed in his response to the king in two ways. "For the man whom the king delights to honor" was the first thing he said to himself, placing emphasis on this phrase. We can see him rolling this glorious thought around in his mind. Furthermore, his response lacked the normal preface that reflected submission to the king, such as "If it pleases the king . . ." (e.g., 1:19; 3:9; 5:4, 8; 7:3; 8:5; 9:13). There was a marked contrast between the attitude of Esther and that of Haman.

What did Haman suggest to the king? "Have them bring a royal robe the king has worn and a horse the king has ridden, one with a royal crest placed on its head" (v. 8). A sympathetic reading of Haman's request would be that this request would honor the king and reinforce their relationship. Wearing the king's robe would have indicated to all the close association between the wearer and the king (see 1 Sam 18:4). Given Haman's position as prime minister, "no other honor was left to him but to share in the king's power, prestige, and stature."[7]

---

5. Jon D. Levenson, *Esther*, OTL (Louisville, KY: Westminster John Knox, 1997), 96.
6. Haman "thought to himself" (NIV) is literally "said in his heart."
7. Karen H. Jobes, *Esther*, NIVAC (Grand Rapids, MI: Zondervan, 1999), 154.

Yet it is instructive to compare how Joseph was honored by Pharaoh (Gen 41:42–43) with what Haman imagined he was requesting for himself.[8] Joseph received the Pharaoh's signet ring, a linen garment, and a gold necklace; Haman desired the king's robe.[9] Joseph rode in the chariot of the second-in-command; Haman sought to ride on the king's horse, garbed in royal splendor. Before Joseph they cried out, "Bow the knee!"; Haman requested a full phrase, "This is what is done for the man the king delights to honor!" (v. 9). Furthermore, a comparison with Solomon suggests that such a parade might have been intended as a succession ceremony (1 Kgs 1:32–40).[10] King David gave instructions for Solomon to ride on his mule, to be anointed, to sit on his throne, and for people to say, "Long live King Solomon!" So to be mounted on a king's mount was closely connected to sitting on his throne.

Thus, what Haman asked for went way beyond how Joseph was honored, and this hints at a grasp for the throne. Remember that Haman already had the king's signet ring. Now he effectively also sought his robes and horse. He might as well have asked for the king's wife for the full house! (He used the words "king" [*melek*] or "royalty" [*malkut*] eight times.) Haman had wealth and position. What he requested was what he still coveted the most: honor and adoration. Indeed, he repeated the phrase "the man whom the king delights to *honor*" four times (vv. 6–9). We get the feeling that his request was moving beyond what was acceptable for even an extravagant and generous king. Haman wanted the honor of a king from the king. So now we reach the point where things took a turn.

Adele Berlin calls this chapter "one of the funniest anywhere in the Bible."[11] Part of the humor in this scene is that the king and Haman ironically talked past each other. The king meant the distinction to go to Mordecai but did not mention this to Haman; Haman detailed the way to honor the person while assuming it is for himself. One effect was that the king's command came as an overwhelming surprise for Haman. The king said "Go at once. Get the robe and the horse and do just as you have suggested for Mordecai the Jew"

---

8. David J. A. Clines, *Ezra, Nehemiah, Esther*, NCBC (Grand Rapids, MI: Eerdmans, 1984), 308.

9. Plutarch recounted an episode about King Artaxerxes, who gave his royal robe on the condition that it not be worn; *Artaxerxes* 5.1–2. Teribazus got away with wearing it because the king considered him a madman.

10. Leslie C. Allen and Timothy S. Laniak, *Ezra, Nehemiah, Esther* (Peabody, MA: Hendrickson, 2003), 239.

11. Adele Berlin, *Esther* (Philadelphia, PA: Jewish Publication Society, 2001), 56.

(v. 10).[12] What a shock and absolute horror this was for Haman! The king even withheld saying to whom the honor would go until the very end of the sentence, thereby heightening the suspense. The honor was not for Haman but for his arch-enemy!

Even more amusing for us as readers (but more painful for Haman) was how the king highlighted the very features of Mordecai that bothered Haman. Haman must parade "the Jew," whom he wanted to execute, around the streets. The king described Mordecai as one "who sits at the king's gate," the very place where Mordecai refused to publicly show respect to him. Haman must call out about the man who refused to honor him, "This is what is done for the man the king delights to honor!" (v. 11). Haman followed the king's command to the letter, following his own proposal. Esther had put on "royalty" previously (5:1), and now it was Mordecai's turn. Haman turned out to be the architect of his own shame instead of honor.

Yet the humor in this scene uncovers an ugly effect of pride: it can lead to blindness. Being so full of ourselves can blind us to what is happening around us. Of course Haman had some reasons to be proud: he had a family and sons to continue his family line, he was elevated to the equivalent of Prime Minister, and he had an invitation to an exclusive dinner. However, if Haman had had a sliver of humility, it might have occurred to him to ask the king whom he wanted to honor. Then things would have turned out very differently.

Haman's situation well illustrates teachings we find in the book of Proverbs. For instance, "When pride comes, then comes disgrace, but with humility comes wisdom" (Prov 11:2). Some of us in Asian cultures are prone to a form of false humility. In front of others we might put down our achievements or abilities, or those of members of our family, yet on the inside we might be proud or self-absorbed. The Apostle Paul tells us that the example of Jesus' life spurs us to true humility.

> Who, being in very nature God,
>> did not consider equality with God something to be used to
>> his own advantage;
> rather, he made himself nothing
>> by taking the very nature of a servant,
>> being made in human likeness.

---

12. Ironically, the king honored someone from the ethnic group Haman had proclaimed an edict to exterminate.

And being found in appearance as a man,
> he humbled himself
> by becoming obedient to death –
> even death on a cross! (Phil 2:6–8)

Having the same humble mindset as Jesus means we "value others above" ourselves and look to "the interests of others" (Phil 2:3–4). Humility is thus the antidote to the blindness of pride.

6:12–14 SCENE 3: HAMAN'S FALL BEGAN

What happened to Mordecai seems strange to us. He was honored and glorified for a short time – minutes or hours at the most. Everyone lining the streets who viewed his newfound status must have been as surprised as Mordecai himself. Then it was all over as quickly as it had begun. Mordecai had his moment of glory but then returned to the king's gate (v. 12). It seems things were back to normal: same old clothes, same old place, and same old job. He received this honor and recognition for his loyalty to the king, but we cannot help but wonder if more is to come.

Clothing reflects deeper realities in this scene, as elsewhere.[13] As one working for the empire, Mordecai wore his everyday clothes to fit into Persian society. When he wore sackcloth, the social aspect of his identity became more important than the personal aspect, as he stood in solidarity with the rest of the Jews in mourning (4:1–3). Here he identified with the king by putting on royal robes, as Esther had done before (5:1). That this symbol of royalty was granted to him by the king strongly contrasts with the ambitious self-seeking of Haman. When Mordecai put back on his everyday clothing, things seem to return to normal.

Things will not, however, be the same for Haman. After honoring Mordecai, he hurried back to his wife and friends, "mourning and with his head covered (*hapah*)" (v. 12; ESV). He had been deeply shamed. In Asian thinking, he has spectacularly "lost face." He covered his head, but others will soon cover (*hapah*) his head for death (7:8). His haste adds to the feeling that he was losing control of the situation. Ironically, the one who had caused the Jews to be clothed in mourning (4:1–3) now had his head covered in grief (v. 12).

---

13. Timothy S. Laniak, *Shame and Honor in the Book of Esther*, SBLDS 165 (Atlanta, GA: Scholars Press, 1998), 116–121.

Mordecai had told Hathach to reveal to Esther "everything that had happened to him" (4:7), and now it was Haman's turn. When he told his wife and friends "everything that happened to him," their response was remarkable: "Since Mordecai, before whom your downfall (from the verb *nafal*, "to fall") has started, is of Jewish origin,[14] you cannot stand against him – you will surely come to ruin (*nafol tippol*; literally, "surely fall")!" (v. 13). It is not just that Haman's friends see that things were turning against him, and they wanted to distance themselves from him. Their advice has a strong, predictive feel as indicated by the change from their being described as "his friends" at the beginning of the verse to "his wise men" (*hakhamayv*; NIV "advisors") by its end. If their previous advice was not wise (5:14), their current words are to be considered so. Reminiscent of Balaam, these wise men cannot curse God's people and bless an Amalekite (Num 24:20).

The word "fall" (*nafal*) in the book of Esther is also connected to Haman and his fate. He caused the lot to "fall" to determine the day to carry out his edict (3:7). King Xerxes told Haman to carry out all the tasks to honor Mordecai, and "Do not let a thing fall (*tappel*) of all that you have said" (6:10).[15] Here Haman's advisors told him that his downfall had begun and he would surely fall (6:13).

We are not told how these non-Jews were so certain of Haman's downfall. Perhaps they knew something of the history of the Israelites. In the Bible, the survival of the Jews bears witness to God's power (e.g., Mal 1:2–5). The Jews still survived when many of their neighbors no longer existed (e.g., the Moabites and Edomites). However, since these wise men already knew that Mordecai was a Jew (5:13), the most likely reason is because they had just witnessed a specific instance of a Jew surviving against all odds. For they had plotted Mordecai's demise, but the Jew ended up exalted (6:1–11)! Actually, all of God's actions – in judgment and salvation – testify to all peoples that he is the Lord (e.g., Exod 7:5; Ezek 36:23). Although Haman's advisors only mentioned "the Jews," the fate of God's people cannot be detached from the action of God. Thus, God's hidden hand can be detected again. Its work was even sensed by these Gentiles, who anticipated the reversal of the fate of the Jews.

---

14. "Jewish origin" (NIV) is literally "of the seed of the Jews," which might be an allusion to the covenants with Abraham (Gen 15:3, 5, 13, 18; 17:7–10, 12, 19) and David (2 Sam 7:21); so David G. Firth, *The Message of Esther: God Present but Unseen*, BST (Nottingham, UK: InterVarsity Press, 2010), 98.

15. Letting "nothing fall" is similar to the description of the certainty of God's word being fulfilled in Joshua 21:45; 23:14 and 1 Samuel 3:19.

Elsewhere in the Bible foreigners recognized then responded to who God is. For instance, in the OT some of these include the sailors on Jonah's boat (Jonah 1:14), Rahab and the Gibeonites (Josh 2:9–11; 9:9–11), Naaman (2 Kgs 5:15–19), and King Nebuchadnezzar (Dan 3:28–29). In the NT, one memorable example is the centurion who declares that Jesus is the Son of God (Matt 27:54).

Then, before he knew it, Haman was whisked away to Esther's next banquet (v. 14). He was in mid-conversation with his close circle when the king's eunuchs hurried him away. He had been "hurried" by the king previously (5:5; 6:10), but now things were really spiraling out of his control. He was about to do more "falling" very soon.

IRONY

Irony is a major literary feature of the narrative of Esther. There are two main types of irony in the Bible: verbal and dramatic.[1] Verbal irony is saying one thing but meaning something different, often the opposite. Dramatic irony is when the readers are more aware of what is happening than the characters. The majority of irony in Esther is the latter; indeed, Esther has been declared "the pinnacle of dramatic irony" within the literature of the Old Testament.[2]

Irony may be hard to detect, and different readers may disagree. Edwin Good presents the guidelines for identifying irony: (1) irony is criticism, implicit or explicit; (2) it may use words with opposite or contrasting meanings; (3) it may understate or suggest instead of making a clear statement; (4) it has a stance, that is, it is not mere opposition, but is protest.[3] Despite these guidelines, Good warns that the one using irony depends on the reader for recognition, and so risks misunderstanding.[4]

How does irony function in the Esther narrative? And why is it used by the author? Irony highlights the incongruity – the difference between how things are and how they should be – of a situation, action or attitude. In Esther irony also reveals that there is justice in the world and that people will receive what is due to them. Sometimes irony is quite humorous, and like other forms of humor, it sneaks up and surprises the reader. Then it ends up presenting the author's intended meaning with greater force. Sometimes an author cannot openly criticize the authorities. In this situation, irony and sarcasm, which is closely related, are used to subtly critique those in power.[5] In the Esther narrative the main foci of irony are the Persian Empire, King Xerxes, and Haman.

This form of subtle critique is found in some Asian contexts because direct confrontation with authorities is impossible. For instance, in Malay culture there is the story of *Puteri Gunung Ledang* (Princess Gunung Ledang). She could not refuse the marriage proposal of Sultan Mahmud Syah outright, so she instead made seven unreasonable conditions that he needed to fulfill. For example, she requested that a golden bridge be built from Gunung Ledang to Melaka, and that seven barrels of tears be filled for her to bathe in. These did not deter the sultan even though her requests burdened his people. However, when the last request involved a personal cost – a silver bowl of his own son's blood – he would not fulfill it. A subtle critique of the king is evident. As is the irony that the king was too blinded to realize that the impossible requests were the princess's way of refusing his proposal.[6]

As we enjoy the verbal and dramatic irony in Esther, perhaps we will begin to see more irony in our world. Irony can make us laugh when things are not as they should be, even when we feel like crying. Hopefully it will point us to a better reality and help us to trust in the one who has the power to make it come true.

---

1. Shimon Bar-Efrat, *Narrative Art in the Bible*, JSOTSup 70 (Sheffield, UK: Almond Press, 1989), 125, 210.
2. Carolyn J. Sharp, *Irony and Meaning in the Hebrew Bible* (Bloomington, IN: Indiana University Press, 2009), 65. On irony in Esther, see also Stan Goldman, "Narrative and Ethical Ironies in Esther," *JSOT* 15 (1990): 15–31, which outlines rhetorical, generative, and intuitive ironies. Some of the ironies Goldman detects, however, seem too subtle to be noticed by most readers, ancient and modern.
3. Edwin M. Good, *Irony in the Old Testament*, 2nd ed. (Sheffield, UK: Almond Press, 1981), 30–32.
4. Good, *Irony in the Old Testament*, 32.
5. Good, 17: "It mocks those who think they are something when they are actually nothing."
6. One interpretation of this story critiques the impulses of the sultan, which resonates with the interaction between Esther and King Xerxes: "Indirectly, this indicates that Princess Gunung Ledang successfully manipulated the power of the patriarchs, who would do anything to satisfy their sexual desires"; Rahimah Hamdan and Shaiful Bahri Md Radzi, "The Meaning of Female Passivity in Traditional Malay Literature,"*Asian Social Science* 10 (2014): 227.

ESTHER 7

The tide that started to turn in the last chapter continues in this chapter. We know things are changing for the better for Mordecai, but we do not exactly know how this will be connected to Esther and her plan. What she started to put into effect with the king in chapter 5 continues in this chapter. There were some positive signals from the king towards both Esther and Mordecai; now it is time to see if and how the reversals will be completed.

In this chapter Esther finally made her request to the king (vv. 1–7). She deftly revealed the crisis for her and her people while ensuring the king maintains "face." The third person at this intimate meal, Haman, covered his face in the previous chapter. His face will be covered again, as he "falls," as predicted by his wife and friends, by being hung high on a pole (vv. 8–10).

7:1–7 SCENE 1: ESTHER'S REQUESTS

There is a Chinese saying that goes, "*wénqígē, zhīqíniǎo; tīngqíyán, zhīqírén*"[1] ("A bird is known by its song, a man by his talk"). We can tell if a person is wise by their actions and their words. As they were drinking wine on the second day of Esther's banquet, the king repeated his offer to Esther for the third time (v. 2; compare 5:3, 6). As Esther finally made her request, there are at least three things we can learn from the way in which she approached the king.

First, she was respectful. She introduced her request with "If I have found favor with you, Your Majesty, and if it pleases you" (v. 3). If we compare Haman's speech with the king in the previous chapter, we will see that Haman used none of these phrases showing submission.

Second, she made the most of her personal relationship with the king. This is particularly highlighted by contrasting her response here with her previous responses: "If it pleases the king" (5:4); "If I have found favor in the sight of the king" (5:8); and "If I have found favor in your sight, O king" (7:3). The more direct and personal way of addressing the king, "your sight, O king" (7:3) replaces "the king/the sight of the king" (5:4, 8). She had been away from the king's presence for a month (4:11), but here we see that she had regained her confidence after spending time with the king at two feasts.

Third, her speech was discerning. By echoing the king's offer, she made it even more likely that the king would agree: "my life . . . my wish; my

---

1. 闻其歌知其鸟; 听其言知其人.

people . . . my request" (v. 3). She alluded to Haman's edict by using the same words: destroyed, killed and annihilated (3:13).[2] Her knowledge of the money Haman offered to the king is revealed by her mention of her and her people being "sold" (v. 4; compare 3:9; 4:7).[3] Esther used a passive verb (*nimkarnu*; "we have been sold") to avoid any hint of accusation with regards to the king's role in the edict (3:9–11).[4] She had clearly accepted and digested Mordecai's plea (4:13–14) because in this situation she identified with her people, so that to threaten one was to threaten the other.

She then continued with a thought experiment. "If we had merely been sold as slaves, men and women, I would have been silent." Why? Because her loss would not compare with the possible personal or financial loss to the king (v. 4).[5] Some of us in Asia might notice Esther's deference to the king, but here we might feel her deference was beyond what was normal. She was effectively saying that the king was too important to bother, even if she, the queen, along with her people were to be sold into slavery. Thus, we suspect that Esther brought up the thought experiment to stir up the shame the king would suffer if this were to happen. After all, he would lose "face" if his queen were sold into slavery. If he did not want that, he had better do something about it!

Just like Nathan when he confronted David (2 Sam 12:1–6), Esther incited the king's anger before she pointed the finger at Haman. She and her people, the Jews, had been sold not only into slavery but to be destroyed. The result was that the king became furious. So hot was his anger that his speech was affected. "King Xerxes asked Esther" (v. 5) is literally, "And King Xerxes said, and he said to Queen Esther." This reflects the stuttering words that follow, "Who is he? Where is he – the man who has dared (literally, "whose

---

2. Ironically, from the king's subsequent angry response (7:5), it appears that he did not pick up the allusion.
3. In the book of Judges, Israel is described as being "sold" to their enemies, like a commercial transaction. See Athena E. Gorospe and Charles Ringma, *Judges*. ABCS (Carlisle, UK: Langham Global Library, 2016), 43–44.
4. This is another link with the Joseph narrative, since he was also sold by his brothers (Gen 37:28, 36; 45:4).
5. There is a dispute about the exact translation of the last phrase in Esther's speech, mainly revolving around the translation of *nezek*. Frederic W. Bush, *Ruth, Esther*, WBC 9 (Dallas, TX: Word Books, 1996), 428, argues for "trouble, annoyance," which yields the translation, "for the calamity would not be worth the annoyance to the king." Michael V. Fox, *Character and Ideology in the Book of Esther*, 2nd ed. (Grand Rapids, MI: Eerdmans, 2001), 84–85, understands *nezek* as "loss" or "damage," which yields the translation, "for the misery we would suffer thereby would not have been severe enough to justify causing the king to forfeit the money the sale was supposed to bring him."

heart has filled him") to do such a thing?" Ironically of course, the culprit was right there in his presence.

Esther did not reveal who the perpetrator was until the king asked, even though I am sure she had been anxious to name him for days (v. 5). The effect of her withholding of the culprit's name was to make the king think about who it could be, as well as to make it seem as if she was not overly eager to divulge his name. Even then, it is only after she had described him as "an adversary and enemy" that she revealed him as "this vile Haman" (v. 6). Her point-by-point response to the king revealed her presence of mind in a heated situation: "An adversary and enemy . . . vile Haman" ("Who is he?"); "this" ("Where is he?").[6] The one who was described as "the enemy of the Jews" (3:10; compare 8:1; 9:10, 24) was now unmasked and rebranded as the enemy of the state. For as an enemy of the queen he was also an enemy of the king. Thus, the way Esther approached the king shows her wisdom in presenting a request. It also reveals her insight into the character of the king.

In one sense, the timing for her speech also shows her wisdom. She could not make her request the first time because Haman was not there. He had to be there because if he had not been, he might have been able to wiggle out of the accusation. Somehow she sensed that the timing was not right to answer the king the second time, but now she made her request. She pointed her finger at Haman. The explosion has gone off. Haman knew he had been dealt a mortal wound. The king stood up and stormed off, probably to the palace garden to clear his head and consider his options. Haman stayed with Esther to beg for his life because he realized that the king had already determined "something bad" (*hara'ah*; "his fate," NIV) against him (v. 7). He knew how the king thought and felt because they were similar in character. Their first response to any threat was anger; their second was to remove the threat (1:12–19; 2:19–23; 3:1–15; 5:9–14). Esther had begged (*baqash*) for her life from the king, but ironically now Haman begged (*baqash*) for his life from Esther. What words might she have used to respond to him?

In many ways Esther measured up well against the description of how a wise person acts in the court of a king (Eccl 8:1–4). As detailed above, her use of words to persuade the king and gain what she desired was particularly exemplary. The last use of her words was to name Haman as "evil" (v. 6). In chapter 2 we noted that Esther chose the path of submission. In chapter 4, after Haman's decree, Mordecai persuaded her to resist the oppression and

---

6. Jon D. Levenson, *Esther*, OTL (Louisville, KY: Westminster John Knox, 1997), 103.

injustice against her people. Here in chapter 7 her choice of active resistance came to a climax, as she stood up to evil and named it.

Sometimes submission is the wise strategy; at other times resistance and naming is required. In India, cases of women naming their sexual predators have gained worldwide attention. Some perpetrators have been brought to justice; other victims have faced repercussions for making a stand. Around the world, the naming of high-profile American men such as Bill Cosby and Harvey Weinstein has sparked a firestorm. Women and men have spoken up about the sexual crimes committed against them. It takes courage to name oppressors and resist "evil." However, sometimes it must be done, especially when it brings justice for many.

This all reminds us that words are powerful. Proverbs 18:21 tells us, "The tongue has the power of life and death, and those who love it will eat its fruit." In this chapter so far, Esther, Haman, and the king would agree with this wisdom. However, we should also remember that Jesus says words are a reflection of what is in our hearts, and we will need to give an account for every careless word we have spoken. "For by your words you will be acquitted, and by your words you will be condemned" (Matt 12:36–37).

7:8–10 SCENE 2: HAMAN FELL

What happened next could not have been planned by Esther. Haman fell (*nafal*) onto the couch where Esther was reclining. Haman's wife and wise men had predicted that he would certainly fall (*nafal*; 6:13), and he did so literally. The act of falling before a superior, prostrating oneself to beg for something humbly and earnestly, is found elsewhere in the Bible, including Esther herself at King Xerxes' feet (8:3). However, here Haman literally fell – onto the queen's couch. Maybe he was begging too hard. Maybe he was tipsy from too much wine. Maybe both. In a darkly comic moment, he toppled onto the queen's couch just as the king walked into the room (v. 8).

As the king fumed outside in his garden he must have been thinking, "What am I going to do? I authorized Haman's edict by giving him my signet ring. Now he has written an edict against my own wife!"

As the king came back in, he saw Haman fall onto his wife's couch, and so a perfect solution presented itself to him. Perhaps his mind flashed back to Haman asking for the royal robes and the royal horse (6:8–9). He put it all together and concluded that Haman now wanted his wife! Treason! Even attempting a sexual relationship with a king's concubine was viewed as trying to usurp the throne. We find similar ideas in OT narratives, such as

Abner and Saul's concubine (2 Sam 3:7–11), Absalom and David's concubines (2 Sam 16:21–22), and Adonijah's request for Abishag (1 Kgs 2:13–25), which Solomon said was the same as asking for the kingdom (1 Kgs 2:22). The same thinking is found in the Greek historians' description about Persia.[7] There is even an account of an Assyrian king castrating his comrade on suspicion of making advances toward the king's concubine.[8]

Now it just so happens that there were grounds for Haman to be executed. As the king said, "Will he even molest the queen while she is with me in the house?" (v. 8). Sexually assaulting Queen Esther was probably the last thing on Haman's mind, but this was how the king interpreted Haman's action, perhaps conveniently.[9]

Straight away, the guards knew what the king meant. They covered Haman's face to lead him away. Previously he covered his head in mourning because he lost "face" (6:12). Again his head was covered, but he was going to lose more than just "face." Conveniently, one of the king's eunuchs, Harbona (one of the king's personal attendants; 1:10), casually slipped in a bit of choice information: "A pole reaching to a height of fifty cubits [22.5m] stands by Haman's house. He had set it up for Mordecai, who had helped the king." The pole Haman erected was visible from miles away, but now its visibility came back to bite him. Previously in the story the king had not made a decision without consulting with others, and things did not change here. We do not know Harbona's motives, but he would have known that his king always sought and was open to advice. Harbona added that the pole was set up for Mordecai, the one who had saved the king's life (2:19–23; 6:3). The king must be thinking that Haman was doubly treacherous: he wanted to kill his queen and one of his most loyal subjects! With Harbona's timely suggestion the king said: "Impale him on it!" (v. 9). We are reminded that the emasculated are not always as powerless as they seem (see also 2:9, 15).

Ironically, Haman was executed for a crime he did not commit. He suffered the same punishment as those who did commit treason against the king (2:23). Yet in another reversal, Haman was impaled on the very pole he had intended for Mordecai. He suffered the shameful death that he had intended for another. Thus, we are not to view this as an act of injustice, because in the Bible punishments fit their crimes (e.g., Deut 19:16–19; 1 Sam 15:23). Moreover, the law about false witness covers intention as well as deed (Deut

---

7. See, e.g., Plutarch, *Artaxerxes* 26.1–2.
8. Xenophon, *Cyropaedia* 5.2.28.
9. So also Adele Berlin, *Esther* (Philadephia, PA: Jewish Publication Society, 2001), 64, 70.

19:19). Haman gave false witness to King Xerxes about the Jews in order to kill them. He falsely accused them of treason, the very charge for which he was found guilty. Haman rightly received the punishment he intended for another.

Previously Esther spoke wisely to the king; now as Haman pleaded for his life she remained silent. She could have spoken up against the king's false accusation. Yet her restraint may again show her wisdom. Perhaps she saw that the king had decided Haman's fate and that she could not go against his will.[10] Certainly she knew that she had more work to do to save her people, and having Haman around would have made it much more difficult. In any case, Haman was not presented as someone who would be open to rehabilitation. Another reason can be drawn from the honor and shame culture of ancient West Asia (see "Honor and Shame" below).

The king's anger subsided after Haman was impaled (v. 10). This was the same sequence of events as with Vashti. She angered the king. Then she was deposed, and after an edict was sent out, the anger of the king subsided (2:1). In both cases the king then felt vindicated. Vashti was replaced by Esther, and we wait to see who replaces Haman.

As we take a step back from the narrative, we see that although it was important for the characters to plan and to act, there were also things which were beyond their control. Esther could not have planned for Haman to build the pole between her first and second banquets. She could not have planned for Harbona to add his suggestion. Certainly, she could not have planned for Haman to fall on her couch just as the king returned. Thus, as we reflect on the events in the narrative, we can perceive that the hidden hand of God was again at work to accomplish his purposes. However, as we see with Esther, that does not mean we should just sit back and wait. We can also plan then act, using wisdom in the opportunities that God gives us. There is a close interplay between our actions and God's sovereignty.

The interaction between God working to accomplish his purposes and our need to act is also seen in our Christian lives. "Therefore, my dear friends, as you have always obeyed – not only in my presence, but now much more in my absence – continue to work out your salvation with fear and trembling, for it is God who works in you to will and to act in order to fulfill his good purpose" (Phil 2:12–13). So in reverence and awe, we continue to obey God each day even as he enables us to live faithful lives.

---

10. Joyce G. Baldwin, *Esther*, TOTC (Leicester, UK: InterVarsity Press, 1984), 93, notes that it was not appropriate for Haman to converse with the queen alone, and in doing so he enraged the king so that "there was nothing Esther could have done to save him."

HONOR AND SHAME

One way that cultures have been differentiated is as being either honor-shame-based or innocence-guilt-based. In an innocence-guilt culture you know if you are good or bad by what your conscience feels. In an honor-shame culture you are good or bad according to what your community says about you, especially if it honors or excludes you. Typically, Asian cultures are considered shame-based, while Western are guilt-based.[1] Yet the division is not quite so neat in reality. Shame is found in all cultures, but the internal form of shame – guilt – is more prevalent in Western societies.[2] Further, although a culture or even a person within a culture may be more oriented towards shame or guilt, both are present to some degree in each culture or person.

Timothy Laniak's study provides helpful insights into honor and shame in the Esther narrative.[3] Honor is associated with authority, obedience, protection, and respect. In contrast, shame is associated with lack of authority, disobedience, disrespect, and public humiliation.[4] The Jews were shamed by Haman's plan to annihilate them. In ancient West Asia, one response to shame is lament, which has elements of grief and sorrow. Laments often also include identification of the enemy, the one who caused the shame.[5] Haman was called an "enemy" (7:6) and "the enemy of the Jews" (3:10; 8:1; 9:10, 24), and those who attack the Jews were called the "enemies" (8:11, 13; 9:1, 5, 16, 22).[6]

Thus, lament verbalizes shame and seeks not only deliverance from the enemy, but also a reversal of status. In chapter 7 we see how honor was only restored when the threat against Jewish lives was removed. In a world of honor and shame, justice can only occur when honor is restored. Honor can only be restored with the death of the enemy. The threat to Jewish lives that came with the shame must be vindicated. Since Haman shamed the Jews, he in turn needed to be shamed – and he was: impaled on a pole, without honor. We will also find out soon in the narrative, a reversal of Haman's intended plan was also required.[7]

The flow of the plot of Esther can be visualized from an honor-shame perspective:[8]

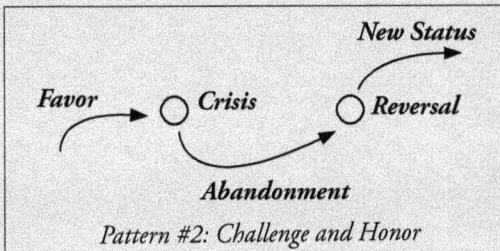

Pattern #2: Challenge and Honor

As we can see from this diagram, the final stage is greater prominence, authority, respect, and honor. This pattern is not only found in the Esther narrative. It is also the same for other narratives in the OT, such as in Exodus, Nehemiah, Job, and Daniel.[9] God is not mentioned in the Esther narrative, but his granting of honor to his people, and his execution of justice against the enemies of his people is the biblical context in which we can understand who is behind the plot movement in Esther.

---

1. As popularized by Ruth Benedict, *The Chrysanthemum and the Sword: Patterns of Japanese Culture* (Boston, MA: Houghton Mifflin, 1946).
2. The rise of social media has created a new type of shame culture. See Andy Crouch, "The Return of Shame," *Christianity Today* 59 (2015): 32–40.
3. To read the Esther narrative from an honor-shame perspective, see also Jason Georges, *Esther: An Honor-Shame Paraphrase* (Timē Press, 2017), available online at http://honorshame.com/HSP/ (accessed May 7, 2018).
4. This is similar to the observation of Lillian R. Klein, "Honor and Shame in Esther," in *A Feminist Companion to Esther, Judith, and Susanna*, ed. Athalya Brenner (Sheffield, UK: Sheffield Academic Press, 1995), 150: "In ancient (and some more recent cultures) . . . the primary condition for achieving honor is autonomy."
5. Timothy S. Laniak, *Shame and Honor in the Book of Esther*, SBLDS 165 (Atlanta, GA: Scholars Press, 1998), 169.
6. The words used by Esther and those used by the psalmists are the same. They both identify the enemy as afflicters and haters and as wicked and arrogant.
7. Laniak, *Shame and Honor*, 170–172.
8. Laniak, 10.
9. Laniak, 7–16.

ESTHER 8

Recently, the terrorist group Islamic State was declared militarily defeated in their strongholds in Iraq and Syria. It has taken three years of fighting to remove Islamic State of Iraq and Syria (ISIS) from their self-declared caliphate. Yet the threat from this group still remains. The situation has been mirrored in Asia. The leader of Abu Sayyaf, a militant group affiliated with Islamic State in the Philippines, has been killed. Yet the threat from this group and others claiming allegiance to Islamic State still remains. Their malicious philosophy continues to spread insidiously around the world, with IS-inspired terrorist attacks difficult to predict and thus prevent.

Haman was gone but his edict of annihilation remained. There was a major turning point in this story, but the Jews were not safe yet. In eight months' time, the edict would be triggered, which, if allowed to proceed unhindered, would spell the end of all the Jews.

Esther mentioned the Jews ("my people") in her request to the king. However, it seems he focused on the threat to himself – his queen and his household. After all, his fury had abated after Haman was hanged. For the king, the matter was closed. The impending destruction of the Jews seemed not to concern him. Esther needed to do something more to save her people.

In this chapter we find that she did. We will also find that the reversal begun in chapter 6 continued with more reversals. In the first scene, Mordecai was promoted in place of Haman (vv. 1–2). In the second, Esther persuaded King Xerxes to allow a counter-edict to be written (vv. 3–8). Mordecai writes the edict in the third scene (vv. 9–14). In the final scene, Mordecai comes out in splendor, and the people celebrate (vv. 15–17).

8:1–2 SCENE 1: MORDECAI WAS PROMOTED

On the same day Haman fell, Mordecai rose. The impaling of Haman probably provided the opportunity for Esther to share with the king "how [Mordecai] was related to her" (v. 1).[1] This information allowed Mordecai special access to the king, the same access previously enjoyed by only a few (1:14), including Haman (6:4). Haman was again described as "the enemy of the Jews" (also

---

1. Literally, "what he was to her" (*mah hu lah*; ESV). Frederic W. Bush, *Ruth, Esther*, WBC 9 (Dallas, TX: Word Books, 1996), 450, suggests this refers to the quality of Esther and Mordecai's relationship, and Mordecai's character, not just their blood relation.

3:10; 9:10) but he had just been executed as an enemy of the Persian Empire. As such, Haman's estate was confiscated by the empire and given to Queen Esther.[2]

The king already knew that Mordecai was the one who had saved his life. When he learned of Mordecai's relationship to Esther, Xerxes elevated him to the equivalent of Prime Minister in place of Haman. The signet ring, which the king had given to Haman (3:10), was given to Mordecai. Mordecai now had the power to act with the authority of the king. One importance of this will be clear soon (vv. 9–10). Queen Esther also appointed Mordecai over Haman's estate (v. 2).[3] He now controlled everything that Haman used to control. The fleeting honor previously granted to Mordecai from the king as he was paraded around the city by Haman (6:11) now had become a permanent reality.

What a swift turnaround! Just the night before, Haman had built a pole on which to impale Mordecai, but during the day, Haman was impaled on it instead. Now Mordecai took Haman's position and possessions. At the start of the day he was destined to hang limp on a high pole; by the end of it, he is looking down from a position of power.

This turnaround is consistent with the biblical view of justice. Mordecai saved the king's life, but he was not rewarded. He is now. By using trickery and slander, Haman schemed to destroy all of God's people but was not punished. He was now. Although God's involvement is not mentioned in this turnaround, we know from elsewhere in the Bible that he is a God of justice. As it says in Psalm 75:7, "It is God who judges: He brings one down, he exalts another." In God's moral universe, evildoers will be punished, and those who do right rewarded (e.g., Eccl 12:14).

We all experience injustice in our lives. Sometimes justice is served in our lifetimes. Singaporean Tan Soy Kiang, 72, was cheated out of S$200,000 from 1999 to 2013. Tan Hwee Ngo, 69, was charged with 169 counts of cheating Mr. Tan by allegedly saying that the payments were needed for Mr. Lee Kuan Yew. It was only when Mr. Tan's niece returned from Australia that she detected

---

2. The seizing of the property of an enemy of the state was recounted in a Persian story by Herodotus 3:120–129. Confiscation of property and impalement was also mentioned in Ezra 6:11: "Also I make a decree that if anyone alters this edict, a beam shall be pulled out of his house, and he shall be impaled on it, and his house shall be made a dunghill."
3. "Estate" (NIV) is literally "house of Haman" (*bet haman*; so ESV, NJPS). Haman's "estate" or property is most likely, although it might also hint at those in Haman's house who will be executed (v. 7; 9:7–10).

the scam and reported it to the police.[4] Sometimes justice will not be served in our lifetimes. Yet we have assurance in knowing that, one day, God will bring punishment and reward for every person: "For we must all appear before the judgment seat of Christ, so that each of us may receive what is due us for the things done while in the body, whether good or bad" (2 Cor 5:10).

8:3–8 SCENE 2: ESTHER PERSUADED XERXES

The arch-enemy of the Jews was dead, but the jaws of death were still open. How will Haman's edict be addressed?

As Esther approached the king with her request, we again see her wisdom. She first appealed to the king's emotion by falling at his feet and pleading with tears (v. 3). She asked for the king to avert Haman's evil plan against the Jews. Wisely, she did not mention the king's role in the matter. Perhaps there was some risk in approaching the king, because he extended his scepter again, a sign of his approval (v. 4). At the show of his favor, she continued by asking him to reverse "the dispatches" of Haman. Again, she started her request with a show of submission: "if it pleases the king." Then she drew on her personal relationship with the king: "if he regards me with favor . . . if he is pleased with me" (v. 4).

Esther's use of words is instructive. By describing Haman's edict against the Jews as "dispatches,"[5] she subtly hinted that they might be reversible, unlike an "edict" (*dat*; 1:8; 2:8; 3:12; 8:8, 9, 17; 9:1, 13). What she asked the king was against Persian custom, and she was aware of this because she added the phrase "if [the king] . . . thinks it the right thing to do" (v. 5). She also intimated that the king did not need to write anything himself by using the passive form of "write": "Let an order be written" (*katab*; v. 5).

She then concluded her request by emphasizing the effect of Haman's decree on her: "For how can I bear to see disaster fall on my people . . . [and] my family?" (v. 6). In other words, Esther said to the king, "If you care about me, you must do something to save my people!" He may or may not have been concerned about Esther's people, but at least he cared about her and the effect the decree would have on her. In these ways, Esther's request to the king again reveals her wisdom.

---

4. Shaffiq Idris Alkhatib, "Elderly Woman Charged with 169 Counts of Cheating," *Straits Times*, June 1, 2017, available from http://www.straitstimes.com/singapore/courts-crime/el-derly-woman-charged-with-169-counts-of-cheating (accessed December 15, 2017).
5. *Hasefarim*, also translated "letters" (ESV).

Also notice what she did *not* do. The official edict was unjust. However, she did not rebel against the edict behind the king's back. She asked him directly. Her submissive and subtle approach ensured that she did not antagonize the king by challenging his authority. In short, she did not try to undermine the Persian system. She worked within the system to achieve her goal.

The king then responded to Esther's persuasive efforts (vv. 7–8). Although Esther had been speaking with the king, he addressed both Esther and Mordecai. What he is about to say will affect both of them, and Mordecai would be the one who would write the new decree. Interestingly, the king said Haman was executed because he "attacked" the Jews,[6] although he was executed on different grounds (7:8). Whatever the case, King Xerxes made it clear that he now supported the Jews.

He also made it clear that an edict written in his name and sealed with his signet ring could not be revoked (8:8; compare 1:19; Dan 6:8, 12, 15). By declaring that he had handed over Haman's estate and executed him, the king essentially was saying that he had done everything he could in the situation (v. 7). He then passed the responsibility to Esther and Mordecai: "Now *you* [plural] write with regard to the Jews according to what is good in your eyes" (v. 8; own translation).[7] How was Mordecai going to "reverse the irreversible"?[8]

Esther and Mordecai's attitude towards Persian rule gives us pause to consider our attitude towards government authorities. The Apostle Paul reinforces the Old Testament understanding that it is God who institutes authorities. Those who resist authorities resist what God has appointed (Rom 13:1–2). However, sometimes governing authorities will abuse their powers. Reading Romans 13:1–7 in the Malaysian context, where Islam is the dominant and official religion, Lim Kar Yong argues that Christians should critically engage with society and government. At times, this may require denouncing practices that are contrary to the gospel, including "acts of corruption and injustice, the erosion of human rights, the perversion of the democratic election process,

---

6. "Attacked" (NIV) is literally "stretched out his hand against" the Jews. Haman did not achieve his aim, but this was the intention of his decree.
7. In Hebrew, "you" is emphatic. This is somewhat reflected in the ESV ("But you may write as you please") but missed in the NIV ("Now write another decree"). The Jews and the money offered by Haman were given to him by the king to do with them according to what was "good in [his] eyes" (3:11). The king now made a similar offer to Esther and Mordecai to reverse what Haman deemed good.
8. David J. A. Clines, *The Esther Scroll: The Story of the Story* (Sheffield, UK: JSOT Press, 1984), 19.

or the promotion of the supremacy of one ethnic group against others."[9] May God grant us wisdom in speech and action as we interact with authorities, whatever our context in Asia.

8:9–14 SCENE 3: A COUNTER-EDICT

There is a Malay proverb that goes, *sekali air bah sekali pasir berubah* ("with each flood the riverbank changes"). A change in rulers and leaders will be followed by changes in rules and regulations. There had been a change in the Persian Prime Minister, from Haman to Mordecai. How was Mordecai going to change what his predecessor had left behind?

First, Mordecai wrote an edict to counteract Haman's edict.[10] The recipients of the edict were similar to those of previous edicts: all levels of government in all provinces in different languages (v. 9; 1:22; 3:12). This time the decree singled out the Jews and their language, primarily because this edict mainly affected them. Yet language is a core ethnic identity marker, as those who live in multi-ethnic societies can attest. In Malaysia, most people can speak at least some Malay and English. To preserve ethnic identity, it is expected that Indian Malaysians speak Tamil, Chinese Malaysians speak a Chinese dialect, and the indigenous speak their ancestral language. It is significant, then, that the Jews could maintain their ethnicity within the Persian Empire, as indicated by the use of the Hebrew language.[11] By comparison, we can see the problem when the Hebrew language was lost: "In those days also I saw the Jews who had married women of Ashdod, Ammon, and Moab. And half of their children spoke the language of Ashdod, and they could not speak the language of Judah, but only the language of each people" (Neh 13:23–24). Particularly important was that the Torah was written in Hebrew, so those who could not understand Hebrew could not keep the requirements of the covenant with the Lord.

---

9. Kar Yong Lim, "Reading Romans 13:1–7 in a Multi-Faith Context: Some Reflections from Malaysia," in *What Young Asian Theologians Are Thinking*, ed. Theng Huat Leow, Christianity in South East Asia 7 (Singapore: Trinity Theological College, 2014), 46.

10. The second decree was issued 70 days after the first. The events between when Haman issued his decree to the events of 8:1–8 is around five days. Thus, there was a long delay from the time Esther and Mordecai received permission to write the decree (8:8) to when it was written. Perhaps the narrator used the number 70 to symbolize completion or perfection. Seventy was also the number of predicted years of the exile (Jer 29:10), so perhaps post-exilic readers would consider the reversal of the edict to be as sure as the return from exile.

11. Adele Berlin, *Esther* (Philadephia, PA: Jewish Publication Society, 2001), 76.

This table shows the similarities in what happened before and after the edict.

	Haman's Edict	Mordecai's Edict
King's secretaries summoned	3:12	8:9
Addressed to satraps, governors and nobles of provinces	3:12	8:9
In the name of King Xerxes, sealed with his ring	3:12	8:10
Couriers went out, spurred on by the king's command; edict issued in citadel of Susa	3:13, 15	8:10, 14

The following table compares the content of the edicts.

Haman's Edict	Mordecai's Edict
The order to destroy, kill and annihilate all the Jews – young and old, women and children . . . and to plunder their goods (3:13).	The Jews [were granted] the right to assemble and protect themselves; to destroy, kill, and annihilate the armed men of any nationality who might attack them, children and women included,[12] and to plunder the property of their enemies (8:11).
On a single day, the thirteenth day of the twelfth month, the month of Adar (3:13).	The day appointed was . . . the thirteenth day of the twelfth month, the month of Adar (8:12).
A copy of the text of the edict was to be issued as law in every province and made known to the people of every nationality so they would be ready for that day (3:14).	A copy of the text of the edict was to be issued as law in every province and made known to the people of every nationality, so that the Jews would be ready on that day to avenge themselves on their enemies (8:13).

---

12. There is much discussion about whether the "children and women" are the attackers' (ESV, NJPS) or the Jews' (NIV). The phrase lacks "their," which has been added by the NIV: "who might attack them and their women and children"; although the NIV places the alternative in a footnote. Based on the structure of the sentence and the parallel with 3:13, the phrase most likely refers to "those of the attackers." For further discussion, see Michael V. Fox, *Character and Ideology in the Book of Esther*, 2nd ed. (Grand Rapids, MI: Eerdmans, 2001), 99–100, 285.

The above tables demonstrate that Mordecai's edict was presented as reversing Haman's one. Since Persian royal edicts could not be revoked, a new one was issued with exactly the same royal authority and support to counteract the first one.

There are, however, significant differences in the edicts. The main difference is that the Jews were allowed to gather together (*qahal*) and "stand up for themselves" (8:11).[13] Previously, they were described as "dispersed among the peoples" (3:8), and thus under the power of the Persians. To be allowed to gather together brings a sense of group identity and collective power, especially since God's people gathered for military or religious purposes in the OT (e.g., Josh 22:12; Exod 35:1; Neh 5:13).[14] The Jews in Esther could use physical force to defend themselves, but only against those "who might attack them." The first edict readied everyone to attack the Jews (3:14), the second readied the Jews to "avenge (from the word *naqam*) themselves on their enemies" (8:13). Based on the context, this does not mean they could take revenge against anyone against whom they held grudges. Rather, this second edict allowed for self-defense and self-preservation against "those who might attack them."

Some of us might find the talk of revenge and vengeance distasteful. As Timothy Laniak points out, however, *naqam* can have a legal connotation. The Jews did not seek just deliverance but "just recompense."[15] The word implies a righting of wrongs. As the Prophet Jeremiah said in an oracle concerning Babylon, "Since this is the vengeance (from the word *naqam*) of the LORD, take vengeance (from the word *naqam*) on her; do to her as she has done to others" (Jer 50:15). Jeremiah called on God to enact a measure for measure response. In Esther, the Jewish response had more to do with restoration of honor than personal vengeance. Until the shame on the Jews is reversed, there could be no justice. Some of us living in Asia today can sympathize with this ancient West Asian worldview. Thus, the Jewish actions can be viewed as not only in self-defense, they are also legally permitted.

---

13. "To protect themselves" (NIV) is the translation of *to la'amod 'al nafsham*, literally "to stand for their lives." Hence, a similar English idiom is "stand up for themselves"; John Screnock and Robert D. Holmstedt, *Esther: A Handbook on the Hebrew Text* (Waco, TX: Baylor University Press, 2015), 221.

14. BDB, 8449.

15. Timothy S. Laniak, *Shame and Honor in the Book of Esther*, SBLDS 165 (Atlanta, GA: Scholars Press, 1998), 139.

8:15–17 SCENE 4: COMING OUT

The contrast between Haman's edict and Mordecai's continues with the responses of the people. When Haman's edict went out, the people of Susa were bewildered (3:15); with Mordecai's edict, the city cried out in joy (8:15). After Haman's edict, he sipped wine with the king; after Mordecai's, there was empire-wide feasting and "a holiday" (v. 17).[16]

The people celebrated not only Mordecai's edict, they also celebrated his coming out in full glory. He wore royal garments of blue and white, a great gold crown on his head, and a robe of fine linen and purple (v. 15). There was a brief glimpse of this honor when Haman paraded him around the city (6:11). This time it was lasting. Previously, Haman was publicly promoted; now Mordecai was.

In fact, Mordecai's promotion was even better. Members of the king's court were commanded to pay homage to Haman (3:2); the whole city spontaneously celebrated Mordecai's elevation. Haman craved the king's robes (6:8); Mordecai actually wore them. Mordecai was honored in a way that placed him alongside Joseph (Gen 41:42) and Daniel (Dan 5:7, 16, 29) – all exalted in a foreign court. While Haman's edict was sent out by couriers (3:13), Mordecai's edict was sent by couriers riding royal horses (8:14; compare 6:8, 11).

In short, the Jews in Susa and in every province celebrated Mordecai's decree and promotion. The description of their celebration suggests that they shared in what their leader enjoyed. The Jews had "light and gladness and joy and honor" (8:16).[17] When Mordecai was honored, so were the Jews. Their happiness replaced Haman's happiness after the queen honored him with an invitation (5:9). Their feasting and rejoicing replaced their fasting and mourning (4:2–3). Indeed, the four words of celebration reversed the four words of lamentation in response to the first edict (mourning, fasting, weeping, lamenting; 4:3). The Jews experienced light after their time of darkness.

Consistent with the rest of the book of Esther, what was behind this turnaround was not mentioned. If we read Esther in the context of the Old Testament, we might find that King David's testimony provides a hint:

> You turned my wailing into dancing;
>> you removed my sackcloth and clothed me with joy,
> that my heart may sing your praises and not be silent.

---

16. NIV: "celebrating." Literally, "a good day," which probably means "a holiday."
17. "Light" brings to mind ideas of "happiness" or "honor" (e.g., Ps 97:11). If the meaning is "honor," the first and fourth terms are in parallel, as are the middle two.

LORD my God, I will praise you forever. (Ps 30:11–12)

Just as King David did in these verses, when we reflect on our experiences we too can often testify that "God is the God of great reversals."[18]

It was not only the Jews who responded to Mordecai's decree and public promotion. Non-Jews also responded. Other ethnic groups "declared themselves Jews" (*mityahadim*; v. 17; ESV).[19] This could mean they pretended to be Jews, or they truly accepted Jewish beliefs and customs. In Malaysia, just like in some other parts of Asia, if a non-Muslim wants to marry a Muslim, they have to convert to Islam. For example, on August 14, 2017, the Sultan of Johor's daughter married a Dutchman, who converted to Islam in 2015.[20] I do not know about this case, but I know of some people who only took on the Islamic religion for the purpose of marriage.

In the time of Esther, the Jews were known to follow laws (NIV "customs") that were "different from those of all other people" (3:8). So did these non-Jews just take on the Jewish name or did they truly accept Jewish beliefs and customs? A couple of factors would support the first understanding, that it was an allegiance of convenience. First, consistent with the reversal motif, the non-Jews who identified as Jews mirror Esther's hiding of her Jewish background (2:10, 20) to promote the Persian aspect of her identity.[21] Second, non-Jews were only motivated by the shift in political power to the Jews.[22] Mordecai had taken the place of Haman as second-in-charge of the Persian Empire. The shift in power had been confirmed by his edict, which aimed to reverse that of his predecessor. Hence, non-Jews only identified with the Jewish people for protection from the coming conflict. Their fear of the Jews (also 9:2) and their fear of Mordecai (9:3) were in dread of their political and military power.

Four factors suggest that some non-Jews accepted Jewish beliefs and customs. First, they did not need to identify as Jews to be safe. They just needed

---

18. Federico G. Villanueva, *Psalms 1–72: A Commentary*, ABCS (Carlisle, UK: Langham Global Library, 2016), 174.
19. *Mityahadim* is only used once in the Bible. This type of verb can mean to become a Jew (as translated in NIV and NASB) or pretend to be a Jew (e.g., NET). ESV's translation is more neutral: "declared themselves Jews" (similarly, NJPS: "they professed themselves to be Jews"). The LXX interprets the conversion as genuine, adding "they were being circumcised" before "they became Jews."
20. Princess Tunku Tun Aminah Sultan Ibrahim married Dennis Muhammad Abdullah (formerly Dennis Verbaas). Johor is a state in the south of Malaysia, which is the second most populous.
21. One of the most prominent aspects of Esther's personal identity is her name. It is thus significant she chooses to use her Persian name, not her Hebrew one.
22. E.g., Bush, *Ruth, Esther*, 448–449.

to refrain from attacking the Jews. Second, the phrasing reminds us of other people in the Old Testament who accepted the beliefs and customs of God's people. "And many of the peoples of the land (*ammey haaretz*) became Jews because the fear (*pakhad*) of the Jews had fallen (*nafal*) on them" (8:17; own translation) is similar to those in the time of Nehemiah who "separated themselves from the peoples of the lands (*ammey haaratzot*) to the Law of God" (Neh 10:28). Third, the response of fear was similar to Rahab's. When she heard about the power of God in the exodus and Israel's military victories, she said to the Israelite spies, "A great fear of you has fallen (*nafal*) on us" and "When we heard of it, our hearts melted in fear and everyone's courage failed because of you, for the LORD your God is God in heaven above and on the earth below" (Josh 2:9, 11).[23] Rahab feared the people of God because she knew their God was powerful. She ended up joining the people of God. Haman's advisors and wife also recognized a power behind the Jewish people (6:13).

In Malaysia, by definition a Malay person is a Muslim, someone who follows or practices Islam.[24] Similarly, in ancient West Asia, ethnic groups could not be separated from their deity.[25] It is thus likely that non-Jews in Esther understood the same reality as Rahab: the deliverance of God's people was a mighty act of God.[26] Fourth, the word "fall" (*nafal*) was used in the Esther narrative to allude to God's hidden providence. It may allude to his working in the non-Jews' response of fear. It is difficult to be sure whether these non-Jews really took on Jewish beliefs and customs or just pretended to be Jews in order to be safe. Nevertheless, on balance it seems likely a group of non-Jews become Jews, true members of God's people.

The phenomenon of people following a powerful leader is a common occurrence throughout history, and something that Jesus was also aware of. As he says: "Many will say to me on that day, 'Lord, Lord, did we not prophesy in your name and in your name drive out demons and in your name perform many miracles?' Then I will tell them plainly, 'I never knew you. Away from

---

23. In Joshua 2:9 the word for "fear" is *eymah*, not *pakhad*. However, they are often used synonymously, e.g., Exod 15:16. For other instances of the fear Gentile nations felt when God was working for his people, see Deut 11:25; Ps 105:38.
24. Article 160 of the Federal Constitution of Malaysia defines a "Malay" as a person who professes the religion of Islam, habitually speaks the Malay language, conforms to Malay custom, and is of Malaysian/Singaporean origin.
25. For example, these were the gods that Solomon worshiped: "He followed Ashtoreth the goddess of the Sidonians, and Molek the detestable god of the Ammonites . . . On a hill east of Jerusalem, Solomon built a high place for Chemosh the detestable god of Moab, and for Molek the detestable god of the Ammonites" (1 Kgs 11:5, 7).
26. In keeping with the rest of Esther, the narrator did not mention the God of the Jews.

me, you evildoers!'" (Matt 7:22–23). Similarly, there may be people in our churches in Asia who are just following the crowd.

The Jews have not been delivered from the jaws of death, but this little phrase, "for the fear of the Jews had fallen on them" (Esth 8:17), hints that God is on their side. Once the God of heaven and earth is on your side, deliverance is a foregone conclusion.

In Malaysian history, the Malayan Communist Party (MCP) was founded in 1930 and laid down its arms in 1989, when they signed a peace agreement with the Malaysian government. Practically, however, the MCP lost its motive for national liberation from the British Empire when Malaya gained independence. As Tunku Abdul Rahman, Malaysia's first Prime Minister, declared in 1961: "When we took over, with independence in 1957, the Communists had been fighting for Malayan freedom. But once we had our freedom their argument lost its force."[27] The MCP continued, with a small number of members fighting at the Malayan-Thai border. However, victory for the Malaysian government was a foregone conclusion after their declaration of independence.

As Christians, our deliverance is also a foregone conclusion. By his death and resurrection Jesus defeated the great Accuser (Col 3:13–15). But sadly, those who do not identify as Christians will not be safe from destruction. There are many around us that we can encourage to trust in Jesus as their Lord and Savior and so be saved from eternal death. We can pray for opportunities to share about the one who has been given all power, and who has been honored and glorified.

---

27. Bruce Boon, *Malaysia: 50 Years of Independence Part 2 – An Opportunity Lost*, November 23, 2007, available from http://www.marxist.com/malaysia-50-years-independence231107. htm (accessed October 3, 2017).

LAND, TEMPLE, COVENANT, KING, PEOPLE

As many people have observed in Esther, there is no mention of the traditional core aspects of identity for God's people in the OT. What might this indicate about who the people of God are?

Although the Jewish main characters in Esther were living in Susa, there is no suggestion that they want to return to the *land* God had promised them (Gen 12:1–7). As anticipated in OT Prophecy, King Cyrus proclaimed a decree allowing the Jews to return and rebuild Jerusalem. According to Ezra-Nehemiah, around 42,000 returned (Ezra 2:64; Neh 7:66). The rest of those taken into exile, including the immediate ancestors of Mordecai and Esther, chose to remain in the diaspora. OT Prophets, however, looked forward to a time with a renewed land with Jerusalem at the center of God's purposes (e.g., Isa 2:1–5; 62).

Any mention of the *temple* in Jerusalem is also absent from the book of Esther. By contrast, Daniel in Babylon prayed towards Jerusalem (Dan 6:10; compare 1 Kgs 8:35–36). The Prophet Ezekiel particularly saw a place for a new temple and worship in the Promised Land (Ezek 40–48). Ezra and Nehemiah, also under Babylonian kings, were concerned with rebuilding the temple and the walls in Jerusalem. The temple was eventually rebuilt and again became the place for the Jews to offer sacrifices and approach God (Ezra 6:13–22). Yet there is not even a mention of prayer in Esther, let alone temple and sacrifices.

In the Esther narrative, the Jews were the inheritors of the *covenant* with the Lord.[1] If we understand the covenant in the OT between the Lord and his people as one core covenant established in stages, then the stages are when the Lord established it: (1) with Abram/Abraham (Gen 12:1–7); (2) with Israel at Mt. Sinai (Exod 19–24); (3) with David (2 Sam 7:8–16); (4) with his people as a new covenant (Jer 31:31–34). In the OT, the term "Jews" occurs in the post-exilic period and translates the word "Judahites," because they primarily came from the tribe of Judah. However, not all were from the tribe of Judah, including Mordecai and Esther, who were from the tribe of Benjamin (Esth 2:5). Some Jews returned to rebuild the temple and Jerusalem. According to Ezra-Nehemiah, they were the faithful "remnant" (Ezra 9–10), the true people of God. According to the book of Esther, the Jews in the diaspora could be just as much God's covenant people.

God promised David that there would be a *king* from his line on the throne forever (2 Sam 7:13, 16). Yet the rule of the Davidic kings ended when Nebuchadnezzar sacked Jerusalem and took King Jehoiachin into exile (2 Kgs 25:1–21). After Cyrus's decree allowing the Jews to return to Jerusalem there was still no Davidic king. Other OT books with an exilic or post-exilic audience look to the fulfilment of this promise. Ezekiel envisages David ruling in the land (Ezek 34:23–24; 37:24–25). The book of Chronicles gives renewed hope by presenting an idealized picture of the greatest kings – David and Solomon. Zechariah looks to Zerubbabel, a governor from David's line (Zech 4; see also Hag 1–2; Ezra 3; Neh 12). The book of Esther may not raise the hope of Davidic rule for a number of possible reasons: the Jews were subjects of a Persian king;[2] they were outside the Promised Land; they looked to God to intervene personally; and it was not relevant to the narrative.

To return to our initial question: according to the book of Esther, who are the people of God? Returning to the land was not required. Worshipping at the temple was not required. Living under a Davidic king was not required. In the Esther narrative, God's covenant *people* were those who were loyal to the Lord. A person could come from the line of Judah and could even speak Hebrew, but a "true" Jew must pledge their allegiance to God's people and, by extension, their loyalty to their God. This was what Mordecai did, and after some persuasion, Esther did, as well. God's people cannot become so assimilated that they give up their relationship with God. There is even a hint that non-Jews can be a part of God's people and participate in Jewish feasts (8:17; 9:27). Loyalty trumps ethnicity in the Esther narrative.

This unconventional understanding of the identity of God's people is consistent with a book on the boundary of the OT. The trajectories found in the book of Esther will continue and be developed further in the NT. After Christ, physical components – land and temple and genealogy – are not essential for the identity of God's covenant people. Jesus, the greatest king in David's line (Matt 1:1), brings in and mediates the New Covenant (Luke 22:19–20; Heb 8:6–13). We, as New Covenant people, find our "rest" in him. So we are not burdened by the requirements of the law (Matt 11:28–30), and we do not look forward to a landed inheritance. Instead, we look forward to our final rest and inheritance in a new heavens and earth when Jesus returns (Heb 3:7–4:13; 1 Pet 1:4). He is the temple who gave us the Holy Spirit so we can worship God in spirit and in truth (John 2:19–21; 4:23–24). The temple in Jerusalem was only an "illustration," a "copy and shadow" of the reality found in Christ (Heb 9). God's people in the OT were those who pledged their allegiance to God – mostly from the Israelites and the Jews. God's people in the NT and beyond are those who pledge their allegiance to God through Christ – anyone who trusts in Jesus as their Lord and Savior (Rom 10:9–13). The dividing wall of hostility between Jew and Gentile has been destroyed (Eph 2:11–18). Haman need not accuse

Mordecai of being different because of the Law (Esth 3:8); in the gospel all ethnicities can now live together at peace.

---

1. The OT speaks of a "covenant" between the Lord and his people, not "covenants" because all the covenants embody the same fundamental relationship.
2. This would be similar to other OT books, such as Ezekiel, which does not have an oracle concerning Babylon, although other surrounding nations are named. Ezra-Nehemiah also does not mention a Davidic hope.

ESTHER 9:1–16

Headhunting was long practiced among some indigenous tribes of Borneo, especially the Dayak tribes, Iban and Kenyah. The skulls were displayed as trophies in the longhouses. This practice mostly ceased about one hundred years ago, although there have been some isolated cases in the past few decades. There were many reasons for the practice, including ritual and ceremonial, for soil fertility and protection, and as a symbol of status and power. Sometimes it was an act of revenge. If one tribe attacked another, they would seek retaliation.[1]

How do we respond when someone attacks us? What if one ethnic group attacks our ethnic group? Mordecai's edict did not allow the Jews to attack any ethnic group they wished. They could only defend themselves against those who attacked them. It allowed for self-defense rather than revenge for previous wrongs.

We will look at this chapter in two scenes. In the first scene, the Jews defended themselves and gained power over their enemies in the citadel, or fortress, of Susa (vv. 1–10). In the second scene, the Jews continued their self-defense in the rest of Susa and the provinces of the Persian Empire (vv. 11–16).

9:1–10 SCENE 1: THE JEWS' SELF-DEFENSE

The fateful day arrived for the two decrees to be put into effect (v. 1). The Jews gathered together in all the cities to defend themselves against those who hated them. These enemies of the Jews wanted to "overpower" them, but the Jews gained the "upper hand": both are translated from the same Hebrew word, *shalat*. It means to gain control or to exercise power over another. People trying to get their own way are a motif in Esther: from Vashti and Xerxes, to Esther and Mordecai, to Haman and Mordecai, and now to the Jews and their enemies. No one could stand against the Jews because they were feared (v. 2; compare 8:17). There is a word play here in the Hebrew: as the Jews "stand" (*amad*) up for themselves (8:11), their enemies cannot "stand" (*amad*) against them because the fear of the Jews had "fallen" (*nafal*) on them (v. 2). The prediction of Zeresh, Haman's wife (6:13), was coming true in a fuller

---

1. On headhunting, see Robert McKinley, "Human and Proud of It! A Structural Treatment of Headhunting Rites and the Social Definition of Enemies," in *Studies in Borneo Societies: Social Process and Anthropological Explanation*, ed. G. N. Appell (DeKalb, IL: The Center for Southeast Asian Studies at Northern Illinois University, 1976), 92–126.

sense than she anticipated. Not only did Haman fall, but those who harbored the same hatred against the Jews would fall also.

Parallel to the response of the peoples, the nobles, officers, governors, and royal officials recognized Mordecai's increasing power, and feared him (v. 4).[2] The leaders throughout the Persian Empire were politically savvy. They understood Mordecai's political power, so they allied themselves with Mordecai's people, and helped them (v. 3).

With the authority given by the counter-edict, the Jews killed five hundred men in the citadel of Susa (vv. 5–6). Now that the Jews had power, they "did what they pleased" (*ratson*) to those who attacked them. Read in the context of war, it means they overwhelmed their enemies, and no one could stand against them (see Neh 9:24; Dan 11:24). Read in the context of Esther, King Xerxes' edict allowed everyone to drink as they pleased (*ratson*; 1:8); now the Jews did as they pleased within the bounds of Persian law.

The Jews also killed the ten sons of Haman (vv. 7–10). Following their father's path as enemies of the Jews, they met the same fate. In the Hebrew Bible, the ten names are listed in two columns.[3] The names may have been arranged for practical reasons, such as for easier pronunciation of these Persian names. Yet the only other place we find the same format is in Joshua 12:9–24 with the list of the defeated Canaanite kings. So perhaps there is a link: both are lists of those who stood against God's people and purposes. As such, their hanging also functioned to deter others who might have considered harming the Jews.

Haman's sons did not suffer punishment for the sins of their father, as those in exile complained: "The parents eat sour grapes, and the children's teeth are set on edge" (Ezek 18:2). Rather, the sons of Haman choose to act like him and so suffered the same fate, just as God says: "The one who sins is the one who will die" (Ezek 18:4).[4] Now all the things Haman boasted about were gone – promotions, physical possessions, and progeny (5:11).

---

2. The description of Mordecai's rise (9:4) is similar to that of Moses: "And the LORD gave the people favor in the sight of the Egyptians. Moreover, the man (*ish*) Moses was very great in the land of Egypt, in the sight of Pharaoh's servants and in the sight of the people" (Exod 11:3; ESV). Mordecai is described as "man (*ish*) Mordecai," and "great" (*gadol*) is used twice in Esth 9:4.

3. The names of Haman's sons are listed in one column, with the other column containing the word "and" along with the direct object marker. For a picture of the hanging scene (although, according to Persian custom, they were probably impaled) from an Esther scroll, see Jo Carruthers, *Esther through the Centuries* (Oxford, UK: Blackwell, 2008), 266.

4. God had asserted this much earlier in Israel's history: "Parents are not to be put to death for their children, nor children put to death for their parents; each will die for their own sin" (Deut 24:16).

We might find it surprising that people still attacked the Jews. Power in the Persian Empire had definitely and visibly shifted to Mordecai and the Jews (v. 4). Mordecai held the reins of government now, not Haman. By this time, it had been nearly nine months since Mordecai's promotion and decree. This is plenty of time for everyone in the empire to have digested the implications and to change their plans. However, there are a few factors for us to consider. For Haman's sons, it would be understandable for them to want to seek revenge for their father's execution. Also, we noticed an anti-Jewish sentiment earlier in the narrative (e.g., 3:8). Perhaps the number of attackers reveals the deep-rooted hatred of the Jews among those in the Persian Empire. Perhaps the attackers were motivated by greed. Certainly, elsewhere in the Bible we are told that the human heart is bent on doing evil (Gen 8:21; Rom 3:10–18). At times this is expressed in violence towards and between ethnic groups. We see this throughout history: the Holocaust, Nanjing, Bosnia, and Rwanda are just a few examples. In Asia, the deadly riots in Singapore (1964) and Malaysia (1969) were also ethnically related. The current situation in Myanmar with the Rohingya people may be another. We find this ethnic violence distressing, but perhaps we should not find it too surprising.

There is no specific mention of God in the Jews' self-defense but there are two hints that he was still working behind the scenes. First, everyone was afraid of the Jews (v. 3). We discussed before how this points to people fearing not just God's people, but also the power of their God (8:17). Second, and closely linked is the phrase "no one could stand against them" (v. 3). Elsewhere in the Old Testament, this phrase points to God as the one fighting for his people and giving "their enemies into their hands" (e.g., Josh 21:44; 23:9). Thus, God is hidden, but again we find hints of his working in this scene.

How does God deliver his people from their enemy in these verses? By a reversal: "the enemies of the Jews had hoped to overpower them, but now the tables were turned, and the Jews got the upper hand over those who hated them" (v. 1). What happened with Haman and Mordecai was repeated on a larger scale. God's people were on the road to annihilation, but then the opposite happened, and they changed places with their enemies.

As we reflect on this scene, we see that the Jews stood up for themselves in response to their enemies' attacks. They did what was allowed under Mordecai's edict – to "avenge themselves" (8:13) or to take "justified retaliation"[5] against their enemies. At times, self-defense as individuals or societies or nations

---

5. Adele Berlin, *Esther* (Philadephia, PA: Jewish Publication Society, 2001), 78.

is justified and necessary. However, although God's people are involved in violence and warfare in the Old Testament, the number of times when God asks his people to initiate fighting is small and for specific purposes. Indeed, God also commands, "Do not seek revenge or bear a grudge against anyone among your people but love your neighbor as yourself" (Lev 19:18). His Son not only taught the same ideal (Matt 5:43–38; compare Rom 12:17–21), but also gave us an example on the cross (Luke 23:34). With the Spirit's enabling, we too seek to live a life of love and forgiveness, and not of hatred and revenge.

Nonetheless, the unity of the Jews is worth considering. Twice we are told that they "gathered together" (*nikhalu*) to stand up for themselves against their enemies (vv. 2, 16). Under Mordecai their leader, they were united in a common cause. Unfortunately, sometimes God's people in Malaysia and other parts of Asia do not enjoy such unity. For example, in Malaysia, churches are often divided along language and ethnic lines, locally and within denominations.[6] There are many reasons for this, especially the easier fellowship from a common language and culture. Yet working at maintaining, developing and displaying the unity we have in Christ (Eph 4:1–6) bears clear testimony to the communities in which we live.[7] Since 2010, the Malaysian government has even been running a campaign called "1Malaysia" to promote ethnic harmony and national unity.[8] Despite the language differences, churches in Malaysia do unite for various causes, especially when engaging officially with the government, under umbrella organizations such as the National Evangelical Christian Fellowship, and the Council of the Churches of Malaysia. Yet ongoing unity within the church, especially the local church, is important in the Malaysian context, as well as in other Asian countries where there are underlying ethnic tensions.[9] Using a common language, such as *Bahasa Malaysia* seems the best way to achieve this. For only the church can demonstrate the true unity among ethnic groups which we have in Christ.

---

6. For example, the Methodists are organized into four tracks: English, Tamil, Chinese, and Iban.

7. For further discussion of Ephesians 4:1–6, see Brian C. Wintle and Ken Gnanakan, *Ephesians*, ABCS (Singapore: Asia Theological Association, 2006), 104–113.

8. See http://www.1malaysia.com.my/en.

9. See Peter A. Rowan, *Proclaiming the Peacemaker: The Malaysian Church as an Agent of Reconciliation in a Multicultural Society* (Oxford, UK: Regnum, 2012).

9:11–16 SCENE 2: FURTHER EVENTS IN
SUSA AND THE PROVINCES

After the report of the killing in the citadel of Susa was given to the king, he asked Esther what she would like to do next (vv. 11–12). As readers, we are surprised because unlike Esther's previous requests, King Xerxes took the initiative. Upon witnessing the Jews' defeat of their enemies, he repeated his earlier questions (5:6; 7:2), but left out the offer of up to half his kingdom. It seems he also feared the Jews; certainly, he knew it was politically savvy to show his favor to them. However, as readers we find the king's unprompted offer a little disconcerting.

Our discomfort continues with Esther's response to the king. She knew exactly what she wanted. She asked for permission for the Jews to defend themselves the next day in the rest of Susa. Esther's request for an extra day was given as the explanation for the two days of Purim, so in one sense it was a necessary event in the plot. Yet because the motivation for her request is not mentioned, there has been criticism of her request for further killing as morally dubious, or even vindictive. We need to consider this further.

On the one hand, she may have had legitimate reasons. Perhaps she sensed that there were still pockets of enemies that needed to be flushed out. She also asked for permission to impale Haman's sons (v. 13). They were already dead, but like the trophy skulls hanging in longhouses, the displayed bodies would have acted as a deterrent, as we discussed earlier. Impaling was a practice of both non-Israelites and Israelites (1 Sam 31:10; Josh 8:29; 10:26), which also humiliated the defeated enemy. Saul and his sons were impaled on the wall of Beth Shan, yet their bodies were rescued and buried by the men of Jabesh Gilead (1 Sam 31:8–13). In contrast, the enemies of Saul's descendants did not have this mercy extended to them, thus compounding their shame and serving as strong warning for others not to do the same. For these reasons – completion and deterrence – Esther's request may have been legitimate.

On the other hand, her motives might have been mixed. In the rest of the Bible, we see that the leaders of God's people are often presented as less than ideal. From Abraham to Moses, from Samuel to David, we see that they too could falter under pressure. In a book with a motif of gaining and using power, it may be that Esther used the power she gained for her own purposes. The author of Esther did not feel a need to justify her action, and so we are left to ponder the moral ambiguity.

As a result of her request, another three hundred men were killed in the rest of Susa, outside the citadel. Perhaps Esther's judgment was proven to be sound. The Jews in the provinces defend themselves, and 75,000 were killed in the rest of the provinces (v. 16). This gives a total of 75,810 dead people. We are horrified by this massive body count. We might start to wonder: did the Jews go too far in defending themselves?

Again, some suggest that the annihilation was required to complete the plot, or that it was a catharsis for the Jews. Some argue that ethical questions are beside the point, since the function of the narrative was to establish Purim.[10] The ethical questions are in the text, however, so we need to grapple with them.

It is helpful to keep eight things in mind. First and most importantly, we need to understand the actions of Esther and the Jews from the perspective of honor and shame. This was an important part of the worldview of an ancient West Asian reader, as well as many Asians today. As Timothy Laniak points out, there is no justice until shame is reversed. Justice is thus closely connected to the restoration of honor. Vindication requires that power be stripped from oppressors.[11] From this perspective, what we find in Esther 8–9 is not primarily personal vengeance but the restoration of honor.

Second, this is a description of war and killing, which is never neat and tidy. One interpretation of the Jews "doing as they pleased" is presented above. Others read the phrase as a sign of "godless license," especially if read with Daniel 8:4 in mind.[12] Perhaps some Jews did go too far. Perhaps some Jews held grudges against their neighbors and used this opportunity to retaliate. This seems possible, but we are not told either way. Third, if Haman's plan had gone ahead, it is likely more people would have died. The exact number of Jews in the Persian Empire at that time is hard to find, but one estimate is that the number was about 750,000.[13] Fourth, the text suggests that the killing was limited to men only, at least in Susa (vv. 6, 15). Although Mordecai's edict allowed for the killing of women and children (8:11), the Jews appeared to refrain, at least in the capital. Fifth, 75,810 was a lot of people, but it might have been a small percentage of the total population of the Persian Empire.[14]

10. E.g., Carey A. Moore, *Esther*, AB 7B (Garden City, NY: Doubleday, 1971), 91.
11. Timothy S. Laniak, *Shame and Honor in the Book of Esther*, SBLDS 165 (Atlanta, GA: Scholars Press, 1998), 140–142.
12. David J. A. Clines, "Reading Esther from Left to Right," in *The Bible in Three Dimensions*, ed. David J. A. Clines, Stephen E. Fowl, and Stanley E. Porter; JSOTSup 87 (Sheffield, UK: JSOT Press, 1990), 46.
13. Joyce G. Baldwin, *Esther*, TOTC (Leicester, UK: InterVarsity Press, 1984), 104. Only a minority of Jews, 42,360, had returned to Judah after Cyrus's edict (Ezra 2:64; Neh 7:66).
14. In the LXX this number is reduced to 15,000. The AT has 70,100 men.

Some estimate there were up to 35 million people at that time.[15] If the numbers killed were exaggerated, the percentage would have been even less.[16]

Sixth, although the Jews were allowed to plunder goods, they laid no hand on the plunder (vv. 10, 15, 16). Looting by the victors was expected in times of war. It was allowed for God's people, except for "holy war" against the inhabitants of Canaan. In those wars, all the people and goods were to be destroyed (Deut 20:10–18). In Esther, the Jews took no spoil; thus, there is no hint that they were motivated by greed. This also indicates that the Jews were able to restrain themselves; they did not run amok. Moreover, if the narrator was making an allusion that the Jews were following the "holy war" instructions, the implication is that God was fighting for them, and this was an act of divine judgment (see below).

Seventh, the narrator was probably alluding to the incident between King Saul and King Agag. King Saul took the plunder following the Israelites' defeat of the Amalekites, but he did not kill King Agag as he was commanded to do by God (1 Sam 15). The Jews in Esther did the opposite: they left the spoils of war but killed the enemy, including all of King Agag's line – Haman and his ten sons. It is significant that Haman's ancestry was mentioned twice in this chapter (9:10, 24) and also that the Jews did not take the plunder three times (vv. 10, 15, 16). This points to the inner-biblical link. Read within the storyline of the Old Testament, what might the Esther narrative be indicating? The Jews finished what Saul should have done and in the way it should have been accomplished. Although there are allusions to Saul and Agag, there are also differences.[17] The Jews did not attack first; they counter-attacked. Also, the Jews fought against attackers of any ethnicities, not just the Agagites. It was not genocide. These differences notwithstanding, the central implication of the inner-biblical link is clear: this ancient enemy of God's people (Exod 17:14–16; Deut 25:19) was finally and decisively killed.

Eighth, on a practical level, relief and peace could only be experienced if the enemy was removed. If pockets were to remain of those who hated the Jews, the Jews would always be worried that they would rise up and attack

---

15. In 500 BC, "one estimate of the population in the Persian Empire is from 17 million to 35 million"; Josef Wiesehofer, "The Achaemenid Empire," in *The Dynamics of Ancient Empires: State Power from Assyria to Byzantium*, ed. Ian Morris and Walter Scheidel (Oxford, UK: Oxford University Press, 2009), 77.

16. Some view the numbers in Esther as exaggerated since the narrative is viewed as fictional, or because it would be consistent with the inflated death counts in the annals of the ancient Near East; e.g., Berlin, *Esther*, 87.

17. Karen H. Jobes, *Esther*, NIVAC (Grand Rapids, MI: Zondervan, 1999), 186–187.

them again. Chinese Kung Fu movies often reflect this practice. The victor kills off whole families to ensure that no one will rise up in the future. In the Old Testament, true peace only comes after malicious neighbors were addressed. For example, in the book of Ezekiel, God said that his people will live in the Promised Land in safety after "I inflict punishment on all their neighbors who maligned them" (Ezek 28:26).

The broader storyline of the Bible adds another perspective to this episode in Esther. Near the beginning of the biblical story, God made a promise to Abram (Gen 12:2–3, 7).[18]

> "I will make you into a great nation,
>   and I will bless you;
> I will make your name great,
>   and you will be a blessing.
> I will bless those who bless you,
>   and whoever curses you I will curse;
> and all peoples on earth
>   will be blessed through you."
> The LORD appeared to Abram and said, "To your offspring I will give this land."

God's promise may be summarized as land, offspring, and blessing. This relates to the Esther narrative in the following ways. Land: the Jews in Esther were outside the Promised Land, although some had returned already under the edict of Cyrus (Ezra 1:1–4; 2 Chr 36:22–23). Offspring: the offspring of Abraham, the Jews, were a people spread throughout the Persian Empire. This part of God's promise was under threat because of Haman's edict. If God's people were wiped out, there would be no possibility for Jesus to be born. Blessing: if there was no Jesus, there would be no blessing for all the peoples on earth. If there was no Jesus, the nations would not be saved. In God's promise to Abram, the flipside to blessing was curse: "Whoever curses you I will curse."

There are two implications for reading Esther in light of God's promise to Abraham. First, God must preserve the Jews to fulfil his promise to Abraham. Second, those who attack God's people were viewed as cursed by God. From this perspective, the Jews took no spoils because they were not acting for their own personal benefit; rather, they were carrying out God's judgment.

---

18. God changes Abram's name to Abraham (Gen 17:5), from "exalted father" to "father of a multitude."

The experience of the Jews as they waited for the fateful day to arrive has relevance for us today in Asia. As the anticipated time approached, we can imagine how the Jews were living in fear for their lives. Yes, Mordecai's decree was written, and power had shifted to the Jews. Victory seemed a foregone conclusion. Yet, would all Jews escape with their lives? Even if they lived, would they still be harmed? How would the day progress? Which of their neighbors would rise up and attack? We can understand the anxiety they would have felt.

Most of us in Asia probably do not worry about our neighbors attacking us because of protections provided by the law. Some of us do fear coming under attack for ethnic, religious, or other reasons. Faced with these situations we might still fear death. Indeed, fear of death is reflected in a superstition found in daily life in much of East and South-East Asia. Countries such as China, Hong Kong, Taiwan, Japan, South Korea, Malaysia, and Singapore avoid using the number four when possible. The word for "four" sounds similar to the word for "death" in some of the languages of these countries. For this reason, elevators may use alternatives for the fourth floor, such as "3A," and when giving monetary gifts, amounts with the number four are avoided. Why is the fear of death so pervasive? Perhaps we are worried that the experience could be painful, or we fear leaving our loved ones behind. Perhaps we fear what might be on the other side of death, or maybe there are still things we want to finish in this life. Whatever the reason for our fear of death, we can take comfort in Jesus. He took on flesh and blood to become like us to break the power of him who holds the power of death, the devil. Thank God that we can now be freed from our slavery to the fear of death (Heb 2:14–15), whatever the level of threat we live under.

REVERSALS

The structure of the Esther narrative reflects one of its main themes. Although there are debates about the details, most scholars agree that the book is structured as a reversal:[1]

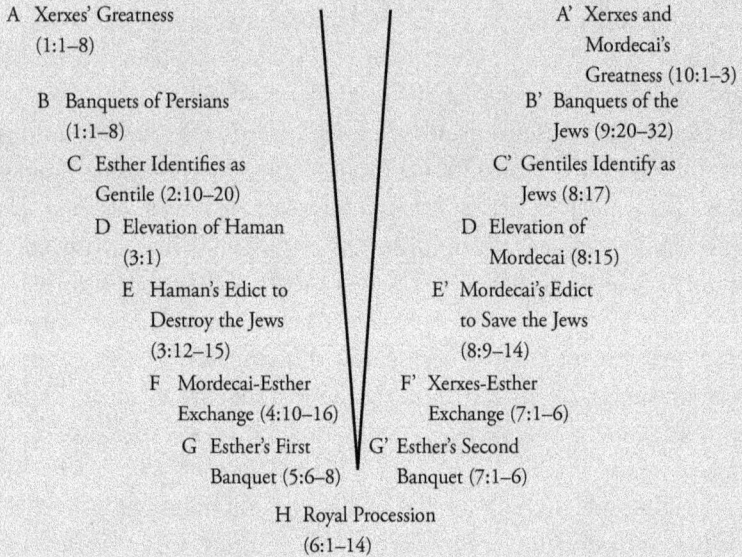

A Xerxes' Greatness
(1:1–8)

  B Banquets of Persians
  (1:1–8)

    C Esther Identifies as
    Gentile (2:10–20)

      D Elevation of Haman
      (3:1)

        E Haman's Edict to
        Destroy the Jews
        (3:12–15)

          F Mordecai-Esther
          Exchange (4:10–16)

            G Esther's First
            Banquet (5:6–8)

A' Xerxes and
Mordecai's
Greatness (10:1–3)

  B' Banquets of the
  Jews (9:20–32)

    C' Gentiles Identify as
    Jews (8:17)

      D Elevation of
      Mordecai (8:15)

        E' Mordecai's Edict
        to Save the Jews
        (8:9–14)

          F' Xerxes-Esther
          Exchange (7:1–6)

            G' Esther's Second
             Banquet (7:1–6)

              H Royal Procession
              (6:1–14)

This V-shaped plot is how the Jews in the narrative (and God's people today) would experience the narrative. Events A to G would be viewed as things generally going downhill after Haman's elevation (D) and edict (E) – the Jews were headed for destruction. There is a minor turning point when Mordecai persuades Esther to act (F), but the major turning point is in chapter 6, beginning when the king cannot sleep (H).

If the structure is rotated a half turn, it becomes A-shaped. In Malaysia I sometimes describe this structure as climbing Mt. Kinabalu, the highest mountain in the Malay Archipelago. A hiker starts her trek from the base of the mountain (A). She continues up the mountain through B, C, and so on, until she reaches the peak at H. The highest point is often something that is highlighted or stressed in the narrative. It is an important section in the structure. Then the hiker goes back down the mountain and experiences things that are similar to her trip up (sections G', F' and so on), until she reaches the base of the mountain again (A'). This would be like tracking what happened to Haman in the plot of the Esther narrative. He started off with low status, was elevated to the equivalent of the Prime Minister of the Persian Empire

(D), and reached his highest point in H, just as the king asked him how he should honor someone. His downfall then began as he was made to honor Mordecai.

The reversal structure is consistent with the working of God's justice. The law of retribution is found throughout the Bible: God's punishment fits the crime. It is also known as the *lex talionis*, as expressed in the Law: "Anyone who injures their neighbor is to be injured in the same manner: fracture for fracture, eye for eye, tooth for tooth. The one who has inflicted the injury must suffer the same injury" (Lev 24:19–20). Haman erected a pole to hang Mordecai; instead, Haman was hung from it. Reversal and retribution is clearly stated in the Esther narrative: "On this day the enemies of the Jews had hoped to overpower them, but now the tables were turned, and the Jews got the upper hand over those who hated them" (9:1). In Esther the principle of retribution is not the basis for personal revenge but for divine judgment through human authorities.

However, the experiences of both Haman and the Jews in the narrative are not completely symmetrical. Haman started at a certain point, rose to a peak, then sank lower than where he had started when he and his sons were wiped out. The Jews started at a certain point, descended to their lowest point, then rose to a higher level because Mordecai became Prime Minister and they gained the favor of all people. This is consistent with the yearning for vindication and retribution elsewhere in the OT, especially in the psalms.[2] For example: "May my accusers perish in shame; may those who want to harm me be covered with scorn and disgrace . . . You will increase my honor and comfort me once more . . . My lips will shout for joy when I sing praise to you – I whom you have delivered. My tongue will tell of your righteous acts all day long, for those who wanted to harm me have been put to shame and confusion" (Ps 71:13, 21, 23–24).

The psalmist wanted those who shamed him to not only be put to shame in return, but also to perish. He looked forward to a time when God would increase his honor. Similarly, Asaph called on God to: "Pay back into the laps of our neighbors seven times the contempt they have hurled at you, LORD" (Ps 79:12).

For both Haman and the Jews, chapter 6 (H) is the turning point. The whole plot turns on a seemingly unremarkable event, King Xerxes' inability to sleep, which triggered a series of unlikely events. Although important in the Esther narrative, at this crucial point the emphasis is not on human planning and action. The turning point was not caused by the actions of the main characters. In this way the structure of the book reinforces the idea of a hidden hand reversing destinies.

Note that God did not intervene in any spectacular ways. There was no miracle, no appearance in a burning bush, no writing on a wall. Similarly, today God works in our lives through ordinary, day-to-day events: the humiliations, the small honors, and the things that just seem to happen. We commit ourselves to God, to obey him and his plan as revealed in his Word, but at the same time we acknowledge his guidance. We may not see God's hand as we live in each moment day-to-day, but as we look back we can often detect God at work gently guiding, directing, and reversing the paths of our lives for his purposes, for our good (Rom 8:28–29), and ultimately for his glory.

1. Slightly adapted from Jon D. Levenson, *Esther*, OTL (Louisville, KY: Westminster John Knox, 1997), 8.
2. Timothy S. Laniak, *Shame and Honor in the Book of Esther*, SBLDS 165 (Atlanta, GA: Scholars Press, 1998), 142.

ESTHER 9:17–10:3

Growing up in Australia, we observed Remembrance Day. Usually I would be at school, and then at the eleventh hour of the eleventh day of the eleventh month of the year, everything would stop. We would be silent for two minutes. It was a time when we would remember those who had fought in the wars, and those who had given their lives to protect our freedom. We would remember the end of the hostilities of war and the peace we now enjoy. We would commemorate the date each year, "lest we forget" war and those who fought in it.

Remembrance Day is not observed in Malaysia, but Remembrance Sunday is observed in other countries in Asia, including Hong Kong and parts of India. World War I and the deliverance from hostilities were so momentous that they are remembered each year on that day.

In Esther 9:17–32 we see that the Jews' deliverance was also commemorated in a yearly festival – the Festival of Purim. How were the Jewish people to commemorate their deliverance? Were they to pause and reflect for a couple of minutes? What were they to remember? Those who had died in battle? What about God? His name is not mentioned in today's passage, just as in the rest of the Esther narrative. So was this a purely secular Jewish festival?

In Asia, most of us who read the book of Esther are not Jewish. We might think that Purim, this Jewish festival, does not have anything to do with us. We might even agree with Martin Luther, who is often quoted as having said: "I am so great an enemy to . . . Esther, that I wish [the book] had not come to us at all, for [it has] too many heathen unnaturalities."[1] If Luther said this, I would like to politely disagree with him. Why? Because looking at how the Jewish people responded to their deliverance can give us some ideas on how we should respond to our deliverance as Christians – for we, too, have been wonderfully delivered.

---

1. Martin Luther, *Table Talk*, trans. William Hazlitt (Philadelphia, PA: Fortress Press, 1967), xxiv. Some scholars argue that he was misquoted, and that he was referring to Esdras in the Apocrypha. Whatever the case, neither he nor Calvin wrote commentaries on Esther. Despite Luther's apparent hostility towards the book of Esther, he still viewed Mordecai and Esther positively.

9:17–22 SCENE 1: THE JEWS CELEBRATE; MORDECAI'S LETTER

The written word was powerful in the book of Esther. An edict was written to authorize the annihilation of the Jews. A counter-edict was written to allow the Jews to protect themselves. Now Mordecai had written a letter to obligate all the Jews in the Persian Empire, both "near and far" (v. 20).[2] They were to celebrate on the fourteenth and the fifteenth of the month of Adar, year after year (v. 21). Those in the rural areas defended themselves on the thirteenth, so they were to celebrate on the fourteenth (v. 17). Those in the city of Susa gathered to defend themselves on the thirteenth and fourteenth, so they were to celebrate on the fifteenth (v. 18).

What did the Jews celebrate? Recently I watched some of the swimming events from the Southeast Asian Games. As soon as a swimmer won, what did she do? As soon as she realized she had won a medal, she celebrated. She celebrated victory! Compare this to the Jews: "to have them celebrate annually the fourteenth and fifteenth days of the month of Adar as the time when the Jews got relief from their enemies and as the month when their sorrow was turned into joy and their mourning into a day of celebration" (v. 22). Imagine the situation of these Jewish people. They had just been delivered from the jaws of death. They had just defended themselves against those who attacked them. It would seem natural to celebrate defeating your enemies.

At least that's how Genghis Khan saw things. He was the founder of the Mongol Empire. By the time he died, his empire included much of central Asia and China, so he knew something about winning battles. This is what he said about being the victor: "Man's highest joy is in victory: to conquer one's enemies; to pursue them; to deprive them of their possessions; to make their beloved weep; to ride on their horses; and to embrace their wives and daughters."[3] To Genghis Khan, pursuing, defeating and killing his enemies were his

---

2. "Near and far" might allude to Isaiah 57:19, in which case Purim can be viewed within God's promise of comfort; so Jon D. Levenson, *Esther*, OTL (Louisville, KY: Westminster John Knox, 1997), 126. Esther 9:20–22 is also similar to Jeremiah 31:10–13, which foresees God's deliverance of his people "from the hand of those stronger than they," when the mourning of God's people will be turned to gladness and their sorrow to comfort and joy.
3. Nina Terrero, *Genghis Khan, Conqueror* (NBC Universal Media, 2014), available online at https://archives.nbclearn.com/portal/site/k-12/browse/?cuecard=68905 (accessed July 25, 2017).

greatest joy – and then taking their goods and their wives and daughters. It was for this he lived. It is what he celebrated.[4]

Is this what the Jews did? Is this how they celebrated? No. Three times we are told that they laid no hand on the plunder (9:10, 15, 16). The Jews did not embrace their enemies' wives and daughters either. In fact, it seems they did not even touch them. The Bible suggests that the killing was limited to men only, not women and children (9:6, 15). Also notice when they celebrated. They did not celebrate on the day of victory, but on the day after.

The Jews did not celebrate the destruction of their enemy. In fact, they celebrated "relief from their enemies" (v. 22). The word for "relief" comes from the same word as the one used by Haman in 3:8 (*nuakh*). When Haman went to hoodwink King Xerxes into annihilating the Jews, part of his sales pitch was this: "It is not to the king's profit to *tolerate* them [i.e. the Jews]." Literally, Haman says, "It is not to the king's profit to *cause them to rest*." This proposal to the king was the spark that lit the flame. The Jews were thrown into turmoil and distress. Now the fire of Haman's hatred against the Jews is finally put out. After eleven long months, the Jews finally enjoy relief and rest.

This relief and rest came about through reversals (v. 22). Sorrow to joy; mourning to celebration; fasting to feasting. Actually, it is one overarching reversal that includes a series of reversals, as we have seen in the previous three chapters.

You might have picked up a dominant note of joy in this celebration. "Gladness," "rejoicing" or "joy" (*sason, sameakh, simhah*) are mentioned ten times in chapters 8–9, and five times just in 9:17–22. Even for Jews today, the Festival of Purim is the loudest and the most fun. As the narrative is read in the synagogue, there is hissing, stomping and the shaking of rattles as Haman's name is mentioned. Traditionally, there are costumes and masks, dramatizations and puppet shows.[5] Why would not the Jews be overjoyed at their deliverance?

This pattern of deliverance followed by rejoicing is found elsewhere in the Old Testament. For instance, Moses and the people sang a song of praise to God after he delivered them from Pharaoh and the Egyptians (Exod 15).

---

4. These practices of the Mongolian army, among others, are described in a recent book by Frank McLynn, *Genghis Khan: His Conquests, His Empire, His Legacy* (Boston, MA: Da Capo Press, 2015).

5. For a brief description of the modern-day Purim celebration, see Adele Berlin, *Esther* (Philadephia, PA: Jewish Publication Society, 2001), xlviii–xlix. The Babylonian Talmud suggests that those who celebrate Purim should get so drunk that they cannot distinguish between "Cursed be Haman" and "Blessed by Mordecai" (B. Megillah 7b).

Deborah and Barak sang a song of praise after God delivered them from their Canaanite oppressors (Judg 5). Rejoicing is a natural response to God's deliverance.[6]

What sort of holiday do we find in Esther? Since the Jews are not described as praising God, is it basically secular, like Remembrance Day on the eleventh hour of the eleventh day of the eleventh month?

Three hints of God can be found if we look more closely at verse 22. First, "relief" or "rest" (*nvakh*) is a loaded word in the OT.[7] God rested on the seventh day of creation, so we "rest" on the Sabbath (Exod 20:11). The Promised Land is promised "rest" from wandering and rest from enemies (Deut 3:20; 25:19). Moreover, "rest" is a gift from God (Deut 12:9–10). Second, the reversal is described in the passive. It is described as "the month that *had been turned for them* from sorrow into joy" (my own translation). This raises a question: What turned things around for the Jews? Or maybe who turned things around for the Jews? Third, the giving of presents of food to one another and gifts to the poor (vv. 19, 22) reminds us of two other joyful feasts in the OT, the Feast of Weeks and the Feast of Tabernacles (Deut 16:11–15). Sharing makes sure that all members of God's community can celebrate, not just the wealthy. Those participating in the feasts included the Levite, the fatherless, the sojourner, and the widow. These groups of people depended on gifts from others. Perhaps the giving of gifts in the commemoration in Esther also reminds people that the deliverance is a gift from God.[8]

These three hints point to the work of God. Consistent with the rest of Esther, God is not mentioned explicitly. Nonetheless, these hints indicate that Purim is not a purely secular celebration.

Giving gifts is important in Asian cultures. There is a Chinese custom of giving gifts in red envelopes (紅包) containing money. They are usually given on special occasions, such as weddings, graduations, and especially at Chinese New Year. In Malaysia, the other two main ethnic groups have adapted the

---

6. Other books of the Old Testament follow this pattern. Songs of praise punctuate the book of Isaiah; Barry G. Webb, *The Message of Isaiah* (Leicester, UK: InterVarsity Press, 1996), 30. Many psalms, as well as each of the five "books" of Psalms, end in praise; see, e.g., Federico G. Villanueva, *Psalms 1–72: A Commentary*, ABCS (Carlisle, UK: Langham Global Library, 2016), 2, 5–7.

7. In the NIV, ESV, and NJPS, *nvakh* is translated as "relief," while in the NKJV it is translated as "rest."

8. Compare Barry G. Webb, *Five Festal Garments: Christian Reflections on the Song of Songs, Ruth, Lamentations, Ecclesiastes, Esther*, NSBT (Leicester, UK: Apollos, 2000), 132.

Chinese custom.[9] The Malays give green packets (*duit raya* or *sampul hijau*) containing money to children and guests who visit during Hari Raya (a feast celebrating the end of Ramadan, or fasting month). The Indians are also known to give purple packets containing money to children during Deepavali. The amount given in the packets varies according to the occasion, but for the Chinese at least, there is calculation required. If you are invited to a wedding banquet, the amount of the red packet must at least cover the costs of your meal. During Chinese New Year, only the married give the unmarried red packets. If you visit a family at Chinese New Year, you anticipate how much the other family will give, and you try to give at least the same amount.

As part of the Purim celebrations, the Jews gave gifts of food to one another and to the poor. The poor cannot give anything in return. The giving of gifts is in gratitude to the blessing of deliverance the Jews have received from God. This is similar for us as Christians also. We give to others, especially those in need, out of a grateful heart. As the Apostle Paul reminds us, "For you know the grace of our Lord Jesus Christ, that though he was rich, yet for your sake he became poor, so that you through his poverty might become rich" (2 Cor 8:9). In Jesus, we have received the richest of gifts, so there is no place for us to be calculative.

9:23–28 SCENE 2: THE JEWS' RESPONSE

In the next scene, the Jews accept Mordecai's proposal (v. 23). They continue the annual commemoration, as they had begun to do already. We are then given more details about how Purim was established (vv. 24–28). Three things in particular are interesting in these verses.

The first is how the festival received its name. Haman plotted against the Jews and cast the lot (*pur*) to find the most auspicious day to carry out his plot (v. 24). Purim is the plural of *pur* (v. 26). It is uncertain why the name of the festival is in the plural. Some possible reasons include: (1) the lot was cast more than once to determine the day to carry out Haman's plot (3:7); (2) the festival is celebrated on two days; and (3) to be consistent with the names of the other religious festivals in the Old Testament.

In the OT, the lot is cast to find out God's will. For instance, Joshua used lots to work out which tribes would receive which portions of land (Josh 18:6).

---

9. For examples of the different colored packets, see Hwee Ling Siek and Tien-Li Chen, "Green Ang Pow and Purple Ang Pow in Malaysian Daily Life Practice," available online at http://design-cu.jp/iasdr2013/papers/1893-1b.pdf.

In Jonah, non-Israelites cast lots to work out who is responsible for the storm (Jonah 1:7). They, too, believed that the outcome of the lots was determined by the gods. So the name "Purim" for the festival reminds the Jews of a deeper reality. Haman thought he determined the fate of God's people by casting lots. But in reality, God's hand controlled the lot and the destiny of his people.

The second interesting thing is that the role of Esther and Mordecai is not mentioned in the recount of the deliverance of the Jews (v. 25). Esther's role in bringing to the king's attention Haman's plot is not mentioned.[10] Although it is also true that the authority for the written orders ultimately derives from King Xerxes, it was actually written by Mordecai (8:9). The main effect of these omissions is to highlight the role of the king, which would be appropriate if verse 25 reflects the content of Mordecai's official letter. But perhaps in downplaying the role of Esther and Mordecai, the verse also subtly hints at God's hidden hand in events.[11]

The third interesting thing about Purim is who celebrates it (vv. 27–28). Three groups of people are mentioned: (1) all Jews everywhere (in every clan, province and city); (2) the Jews' offspring; and (3) all those who joined the Jews. The Jews are to keep Purim and to pass it on to their children. They are to keep the festival so the memory of what happened will not die out. This is similar to Deuteronomy 6:20–25, where parents are commanded to pass on the memory of God's deliverance in the Exodus to the next generation. As we see in Israel's history, not passing on the memory of God's mighty deeds to the next generation can have disastrous consequences (e.g., Judg 2:10–15). Viewed within the context of the OT, passing on the memory of God's deliverance from one generation to the next is not so surprising.

The third group of people who celebrate Purim is perhaps unexpected. They are "all who joined (*hannilvim*) them." Who are these people who joined the Jews? Previously it was not clear if those who called themselves Jews were genuine Jews or not (8:17). Here there is more certainty. The Hebrew word used is the same one used in Isaiah 56:6, "And foreigners who bind themselves (*hannilvim*) to the LORD to minister to him, to love the name of the LORD, and to be his servants." Those who join the Jews in celebrating Purim are

---

10. The phrase is literally "And when she/it came before the king." Who or what "she/it" (feminine) refers to is ambiguous. It is unlikely to refer to Esther because she has not been mentioned since 9:13. It most probably refers to "Haman's evil scheme," which is mentioned just later in verse 25. For further discussion, see Frederic W. Bush, *Ruth, Esther*, WBC 9 (Dallas, TX: Word Books, 1996), 481–482.
11. David G. Firth, *The Message of Esther: God Present but Unseen*, BST (Nottingham, UK: InterVarsity Press, 2010), 135.

foreigners who are incorporated into God's people. Most, if not all, of these people probably come from the same group of foreigners mentioned previously in the narrative (8:17).

This continues a theme found in the rest of the Old Testament. Outsiders joining God's people is seen in the mixed multitude that left Egypt with the Israelites (Exod 12:38) after God displayed his power in the Exodus (compare Exod 12:16; Ps 105:38). These outsiders participated in another religious festival – the Passover (Exod 12:48–49). Sojourners joined God's people in their other religious events in the Promised Land, e.g., the festivals of Weeks and of Tabernacles (Deut 16:9–15). When some Jews returned to the Promised Land, outsiders also joined in celebrating the Passover (Ezra 6:19–21; Neh 10:28).[12] Significantly, the Esther narrative is set outside the Promised Land, but the historical setting overlaps with Ezra-Nehemiah. In the post-exilic period, outsiders could join God's people, even in the diaspora. Throughout the Old Testament, God has been open to outsiders joining his people, in particular to those who respond to him in the correct way.

As we reflect on this scene in Esther, we again notice that there is no mention of God. But reading the scene within the wider context of the Old Testament helps us see the hints pointing to God – his hidden hand, his mighty act of deliverance, his openness to outsiders. Purim is not a godless celebration.

9:29–32 SCENE 3: ESTHER'S LETTER

In the next scene, Esther writes an official letter to confirm the celebration of Purim (vv. 29–32). As "Queen Esther" she uses her royal authority to add weight to Mordecai's letter (v. 29). In one sense, this extra authority is needed, since this is the only religious festival in the Old Testament that is not directly instituted by God. She writes words of "goodwill and assurance" (*shalom veemet*; translated "peace and truth" in ESV, NKJV), which either refers to the tone of her letter or, more likely, to the content of her letter (see also 10:3).

Esther adds a wrinkle to our understanding of Purim. In verse 31, she mentions "times of fasting and lamentation." It might seem that lamenting is out of place for a festival with a strong note of joy. But fasting and lamenting helps the Jews to remember their situation before their deliverance (see 4:3, 16). Those of us living in Asian countries with Muslim neighbors can see that

---

12. For a discussion of the incorporation of non-Jews into God's people in Ezra-Nehemiah, see Peter H. W. Lau, "Gentile Incorporation into Israel in Ezra–Nehemiah?," *Bib* 90 (2009): 356–373.

they follow a similar progression – from fasting to celebration. The end of the Islamic fasting month of Ramadan is celebrated with the holiday of *Eid al-Fitr*. In Malaysia, during *Hari Raya* ("celebration day") *Aidilfitri*, Muslim houses are open for feasting, to Muslim and often non-Muslim neighbors alike. The progression from fasting to feasting in the Jewish celebration of Purim highlights the reversal, giving God's people a greater appreciation of their celebration and joy.

10:1–3 SCENE 4: MORDECAI'S GREATNESS

Our narrative ends with reminders of its beginning. We are again reminded of the power and reach of the Persian Empire. It has the power to grant a suspension of work or taxes (2:18). It has the power to re-impose taxes or forced labor on all under its power, all the way to the distant coastlands (on the eastern Mediterranean; 10:1).

Just like at the beginning of the Esther narrative, the Persian king's "power and might" is mentioned (v. 2). In other parts of the OT, it is to God alone that "power and might" belongs (e.g., 1 Chr 29:12; 2 Chr 20:6).[13] So this might be a hint that God gives power to people to achieve his purposes. In any case, the authenticity of Mordecai's greatness can be found in the historical records of the kings of Media and Persia, no less (v. 2; see also 2:23; 6:1). Elsewhere in the Old Testament, the actions of the kings of Israel and Judah are recorded in historical records (e.g., "the book of the Chronicles of the kings of Judah" [1 Kgs 14:29]). It is almost as if Mordecai is raised to the same status as the Israelite kings. He is, after all, the leader of the Jews spread throughout the whole known world at the time.

The Persian Empire might be magnificent, but its king has shared some of that honor with Mordecai (v. 3). He is only answerable to the king, just as Joseph was to Pharaoh in Egypt (Gen 41:40). Unlike Haman, however, Mordecai did not seek power for his own benefit. He did not use his power to oppress others. Instead, Mordecai worked for the good of his people, God's people. He also spoke "peace" (*shalom*) to all his people. "Rest" or "relief" from enemies has been won (9:16, 22). Now the other side of the coin, "peace" can also be enjoyed. In Old Testament thinking, peace is not just a time of no war. It is a state of well-being, wholeness and positive relationships. This rest and

---

13. It is also true in the NT; compare Revelation 7:12, "Praise and glory and wisdom and thanks and honor and power and strength be to our God forever and ever."

peace is in contrast with what Haman brought to the people. He only brought distress and confusion (e.g., 3:15).

Nonetheless, when we reflect on this ending to the Esther narrative, we might find it a little unsatisfactory. Mordecai is second only to the Persian king, but a foreign Persian king still rules over the Jews. Indeed, he is still taxing the Jews (10:1).[14] Although some of us might not like taxes, like the Sales and Services Tax and other taxes in Malaysia, or the taxes wherever you live, you can be sure that King Xerxes' taxes or tribute were even more onerous.

And although Mordecai is built up to be like the Israelite kings, in reality he is not. He is not even from David's line, the line of the Messiah. Maybe you are thinking, "At least Mordecai brought rest and peace for his people." That is true. But for how long? How long will it be before another sinister Haman-type comes to bring oppression and suffering for God's people? Someone, say, like King Herod (Matt 2:16–18)?

The ending of this story is like an unfinished symphony. Unsatisfying.

If you listen to classical music, you may have heard Franz Schubert's Symphony No. 8. It is commonly known as the "Unfinished Symphony." Recently, I went to a concert where it was performed by the *Orkestra Simfoni Kebangsaan Malaysia* (Malaysian National Symphony Orchestra). When the orchestra played the last note of the third movement, I said to my son, "That sounds pretty final. Why is it called 'unfinished'?" On one level, it was finished. But for those in the know, a symphony should have four movements. Although Schubert lived another six years, he never finished this symphony. Over the years, you can imagine what people have done. They have written alternative movements in the style of Schubert to finish it off for him.

The book of Esther is finished in one sense. However, for those in the know, it is unfinished. Its ending is unsatisfying, with loose ends still to be tied. Another movement needed to be composed.

And it has been. Five hundred years later, Jesus said, "Come to me, all you who are weary and burdened, and I will give you rest. Take my yoke upon you and learn from me, for I am gentle and humble in heart, and you will find rest for your souls. For my yoke is easy and my burden is light" (Matt 11:28–30).

As Christians, Jesus has delivered us from our enemies: Satan, sin and death. This was the greatest deliverance and the ultimate reversal. We are delivered so that we, just like the Jews, can enjoy rest and peace. As Christians, our rest is now primarily spiritual. It is a rest for our souls. We can rest from the

---

14. The Hebrew word *mas* is translated as "tax" (ESV) or "tribute" (NIV, NJPS).

guilt of our sin. We can rest from the burden of trying to earn our salvation. Just as the Jews in Persia did not have to find rest in the physical Promised Land, we do not need to either.

The other side of "rest" is "peace." As the Apostle Paul tells us, Jesus is our peace (Eph 2:11–22). In Jesus, there is now no animosity between Jew and Gentile. Pope Francis recently visited Myanmar. In a context of hostility between ethnic groups, he spoke these words: "The future of Myanmar must be peace, a peace based on respect for the dignity and rights of each member of society, respect for each ethnic group and its identity, respect for the rule of law, and respect for a democratic order that enables each individual and every group – none excluded – to offer its legitimate contribution to the common good."[15] The resolution of the ethnic conflict, along with genuine and lasting peace might seem far off in Myanmar and other parts of the world. Yet Jesus has preached peace to us who were far off. Those of us who are Gentiles have now been brought near by the blood of Christ. Through Jesus we are now fellow citizens in the kingdom of Christ. We can enjoy well-being, wholeness and positive relationships with all peoples.

So Jesus is like a better Mordecai. Jesus gives us true peace. Jesus is the one who truly seeks our welfare. Jesus is the one who speaks peace to us, his people – a lasting peace.

---

15. See http://w2.vatican.va/content/francesco/en/speeches/2017/november/documents/papa-francesco_20171128_viaggioapostolico-myanmar-autorita.html (accessed November 28, 2017).

RESPONDING TO DELIVERANCE

Like the Jews in Esther, there are two main ways in which we should respond to God's deliverance: remember and rejoice.

As Christians, we do not celebrate God's deliverance of the Jews each year in the Festival of Purim. Instead, we *remember* the wonderful deliverance we have in Christ. In a sense, all of God's deliverances of his people in the OT anticipate the greatest deliverance in Jesus. Easter, when we remember the ultimate reversal, is our closest yearly commemoration. Some Christian denominations in Asia, like the Anglicans and the Methodists, have yearly festivals and seasons to help people remember what God has done. Along with Easter, there is also Christmas. Before these seasons come Lent and Advent as times of repentance, preparation and anticipation. These annual cycles help people to remember God's mighty deeds of deliverance. We also have the Lord's Supper. We celebrate it more often than yearly, but in it we also remember our deliverance through Jesus' death.

God knows our human nature and that we tend to forget what he has done for us. We all have spiritual amnesia. These sacraments, festivals, seasons, and cycles in the church calendar help us to remember.

Even this, however, could lead to another problem. If these celebrations and cycles become just a routine, something we just do, they could lose their meanings. We need to reflect continually on what God has done in delivering us. That should be our first response to God's deliverance: to remember.

Our second response to our deliverance should be to *rejoice*. This is what the Apostle Peter wrote (1 Pet 1:8–9):

> Though you have not seen him, you love him; and even though you do not see him now, you believe in him and are filled with an inexpressible and glorious joy, for you are receiving the end result of your faith, the salvation of your souls.

Like in the Festival of Purim, our lives should be bursting with gladness and joy! Three Muslim-majority countries, including two Asian ones (Brunei and Tajikistan), recently banned the public celebration of Christmas.[1] Yet as we feast and celebrate at Christmas each year (privately or publicly), our celebrations should be the most joyous of everyone in Asia, and, as we live from day-to-day, our lives should be marked by an inexpressible joy because we are saved.

So, how would we describe ourselves? Joyful or mournful? Glad or grumpy? What are things in our lives which thrill us? Does our family see us rejoicing in God's mighty acts? Do our friends and colleagues hear us delight in our deliverance?

I think we often are not joyful because we have forgotten about our deliverance. We make long to-do lists each day. (At least I do.) We think that ticking off all the items will make us be satisfied and glad. From this Bible passage, however, there's one thing we should write at the top of our lists to make us truly joyful: "remember deliverance."

As we remember God's greatest deliverance through the ultimate reversal may others see our joy and join us as citizens in the kingdom of Christ.

1. Nicky Woolf, "Christmas Celebrations Banned in Somalia, Tajikistan and Brunei," *The Guardian*, December 23, 2015.

BIBLIOGRAPHY

Alkhatib, Shaffiq Idris. "Elderly Woman Charged with 169 Counts of Cheating." *Straits Times*, June 1, 2017. Online: http://www.straitstimes.com/singapore/ courts-crime/elderly-woman-charged-with-169-counts-of-cheating.

Allen, Leslie C., and Timothy S. Laniak. *Ezra, Nehemiah, Esther*. Peabody, MA: Hendrickson, 2003.

Alter, Robert. *The Art of Biblical Narrative*. New York, NY: Basic Books, 1981.

Baldwin, Joyce G. *Esther*. TOTC. Leicester, UK: InterVarsity Press, 1984.

Bar-Efrat, Shimon. *Narrative Art in the Bible*. JSOTSup 70. Sheffield, UK: Almond Press, 1989.

Bartholomew, Craig G., and Michael W. Goheen. *The Drama of Scripture: Finding Our Place in the Biblical Story*. Grand Rapids, MI: Baker Academic, 2004.

Bauckham, Richard. *The Bible in Politics: How to Read the Bible Politically*. 2nd ed. London, UK: SPCK, 2010.

Bendor, Shunya. *The Social Structure of Ancient Israel: The Institution of the Family (beit 'ab) from the Settlement to the End of the Monarchy*. Jerusalem Biblical Studies 7. Jerusalem, Israel: Simor, 1996.

Benedict, Ruth. *The Chrysanthemum and the Sword: Patterns of Japanese Culture*. Boston, MA: Houghton Mifflin, 1946.

Berlin, Adele. *Esther*. Philadelphia, PA: Jewish Publication Society, 2001.

———. *Poetics and Interpretation of Biblical Narrative*. Sheffield, UK: Almond Press, 1983.

Boon, Bruce. *Malaysia: 50 Years of Independence Part 2 – An Opportunity Lost*. November 23, 2007. Online: http://www.marxist.com/malaysia-50-years independence231107.htm.

Bush, Frederic W. *Ruth, Esther*. WBC 9. Dallas, TX: Word Books, 1996.

Carruthers, Jo. *Esther through the Centuries*. Oxford, UK: Blackwell, 2008.

Chan, Simon. *Grassroots Asian Theology: Thinking the Faith from the Ground Up*. Downers Grove, IL: InterVarsity Press, 2014.

Clarence, David. "Esther." In *South Asia Bible Commentary: A One-Volume Commentary on the Whole Bible*, edited by Brian C. Wintle, 567–578. Grand Rapids, MI: Zondervan, 2015.

Clines, David J. A. "Reading Esther from Left to Right." In *The Bible in Three Dimensions*, edited by David J. A. Clines, Stephen E. Fowl and Stanley E. Porter, 31–52. Sheffield, UK: JSOT Press, 1990.

———. *The Esther Scroll: The Story of the Story*. Sheffield, UK: JSOT Press, 1984.

———. *Ezra, Nehemiah, Esther*. NCBC. Grand Rapids, MI: Eerdmans, 1984.

Crouch, Andy. "The Return of Shame." *Christianity Today* 59 (2015): 32–40.

Dandamayev, Muhammad. "Eunuchs, Archemenid Period." In *Encyclopædia Iranica*. Online: http://www.iranicaonline.org/articles/eunuchs.

Day, Linda M. *Esther*. Abingdon Old Testament Commentaries. Nashville, TN: Abingdon Press, 2005.

Enriquez, Amee. "Philippines: How to Make a Beauty Queen." In *BBC News*, February 2, 2014. Online: http://www.bbc.com/news/world-asia-25550425.

Firth, David G. *The Message of Esther: God Present but Unseen*. BST. Nottingham, UK: InterVarsity Press, 2010.

Fox, Michael V. *Character and Ideology in the Book of Esther*. 2nd ed. Grand Rapids, MI: Eerdmans, 2001.

———. *Character and Ideology in the Book of Esther*. Columbia, SC: University of South Carolina Press, 1991.

Georges, Jason. *Esther: An Honor-Shame Paraphrase*. Online: http://honorshame. com/HSP/. Timē Press, 2017.

Goldman, Stan. "Narrative and Ethical Ironies in Esther." *JSOT* 15 (1990): 15–31.

Good, Edwin M. *Irony in the Old Testament*. 2nd ed. Sheffield, UK: Almond Press, 1981.

Gordis, Robert. "Studies in the Esther Narrative." *JBL* 95 (1976): 43–58.

Gorospe, Athena E., and Charles Ringma. *Judges*. ABCS. Carlisle, UK: Langham Global Library, 2016.

Goswell, Greg. "Keeping God Out of the Book of Esther." *EvQ* 82 (2010): 99–110.

Grossman, Yonatan. "The Vanishing Character in Biblical Narrative: The Role of Hathach in Esther 4." *VT* 62 (2012): 561–571.

Hamdan, Rahimah, and Shaiful Bahri Md Radzi. "The Meaning of Female Passivity in Traditional Malay Literature." *Asian Social Science* 10 (2014): 222–228.

Harper, Prudence Oliver, Joan Aruz, and Françoise Tallon. *The Royal City of Susa: Ancient Near Eastern Treasures in the Louvre*. New York, NY: Metropolitan Museum of Art, 1992.

Haslam, S. Alexander, Stephen Reicher, and Michael Platow. *The New Psychology of Leadership: Identity, Influence, and Power*. Hove, UK: Psychology Press, 2011.

Hazony, Yoram. *God and Politics in Esther*. 2nd ed. Cambridge, UK: Cambridge University Press, 2016.

Huot, Jean-Louis. "Xerxes I." In *Encyclopædia Britannica*. Online: https://www. britannica.com/biography/Xerxes-I.

Jobes, Karen H. *Esther*. NIVAC. Grand Rapids, MI: Zondervan, 1999.

Klein, Lillian R. "Honor and Shame in Esther." In *A Feminist Companion to Esther, Judith, and Susanna*, edited by Athalya Brenner, 149–175. Sheffield, UK: Sheffield Academic Press, 1995.

Kuan, Jeffrey Kah-Jin. "Diasporic Reading of a Diasporic Text: Identity Politics and Race Relations and the Book of Esther." In *Interpreting Beyond Borders*, edited by Fernando F. Segovia, 161–173. Sheffield, UK: Sheffield Academic Press, 2000.

Laniak, Timothy S. *Shame and Honor in the Book of Esther*. SBLDS 165. Atlanta, GA: Scholars Press, 1998.

Lau, Peter H. W. "Gentile Incorporation into Israel in Ezra-Nehemiah? *Bib* 90 (2009): 356–373.

Lee, Raymond L. M. "Continuity and Change in Chinese Spirit Mediumship in Urban Malaysia." *Bijdragen tot de Taal-, Land-en Volkenkunde* 142 (1986): 198–214.

Levenson, Jon D. *Esther*. OTL. Louisville, KY: Westminster John Knox, 1997.

Lim, Kar Yong. "Reading Romans 13:1–7 in a Multi-Faith Context: Some Reflections from Malaysia." In *What Young Asian Theologians Are Thinking*, edited by Theng Huat Leow, 37–47. Singapore: Trinity Theological College, 2014.

Linafelt, Tod, and Timothy K. Beal. *Ruth & Esther*. Berit Olam. Collegeville, MN: Liturgical Press, 1999.

Luther, Martin. *Table Talk*. Translated by William Hazlitt. Philadelphia, PA: Fortress Press, 1967.

McKinley, Robert. "Human and Proud of It! A Structural Treatment of Headhunting Rites and the Social Definition of Enemies." In *Studies in Borneo Societies: Social Process and Anthropological Explanation*, edited by G. N. Appell, 92–126. DeKalb, IL: The Center for Southeast Asian Studies at Northern Illinois University, 1976.

McLynn, Frank. *Genghis Khan: His Conquests, His Empire, His Legacy*. Boston, MA: Da Capo Press, 2015.

Moore, Carey A. *Esther*. AB 7B. Garden City, NY: Doubleday, 1971.

Nor, Hilmy. *Circumcised Heart*. Petaling Jaya, Malaysia: Kairos Research Centre, 1999.

Paton, Lewis B. *A Critical and Exegetical Commentary on the Book of Esther*. Edinburgh, UK: T&T Clark, 1976.

Pierce, Ronald W. "The Politics of Esther and Mordecai: Courage or Compromise?" *BBR* 2 (1992): 75–89.

Provan, Iain W., V. Philips Long, and Tremper Longman. *A Biblical History of Israel*. 2nd ed. Louisville, KY: Westminster John Knox, 2015.

Queen-Sutherland, Kandy. *Ruth and Esther*. Macon, GA: Smyth & Helwys, 2016.

Roberts, Vaughan. *God's Big Picture: Tracing the Storyline of the Bible*. Leicester, UK: InterVarsity Press, 2003.

Rowan, Peter A. *Proclaiming the Peacemaker: The Malaysian Church as an Agent of Reconciliation in a Multicultural Society*. Oxford, UK: Regnum, 2012.

Schmitt, R. "Achaemenid Dynasty," *Encyclopædia Iranica*. Online: http://www.iranicaonline.org/articles/achaemenid-dynasty.

Screnock, John, and Robert D. Holmstedt. *Esther: A Handbook on the Hebrew Text.* Waco, TX: Baylor University Press, 2015.

Sechiyama, Kaku. *Patriarchy in East Asia: A Comparative Sociology of Gender.* Translated by James Smith. Leiden, Netherlands: Brill, 2013.

Sharp, Carolyn J. *Irony and Meaning in the Hebrew Bible.* Bloomington, IN: Indiana University Press, 2009.

Siek, Hwee Ling, and Tien-Li Chen. "Green Ang Pow and Purple Ang Pow in Malaysian Daily Life Practice." National Taipei University of Technology. Online: http://design-cu.jp/iasdr2013/papers/1893-1b.pdf.

Song, Angeline. "Heartless Bimbo or Subversive Role Model?: A Narrative (Self) Critical Reading of the Character of Esther." *Dialog* 49 (2010): 56–69.

Steer, Roger. *J. Hudson Taylor: A Man in Christ.* Milton Keynes, UK: Authentic Publishing, 2001.

Terrero, Nina. *Genghis Khan, Conqueror.* NBC Universal Media, 2014. Online: https://archives.nbclearn.com/portal/site/k-12/browse/?cuecard=68905.

Vaux, Roland de. *Ancient Israel: Its Life and Institutions.* Translated by John McHugh. 2nd ed. London, UK: Dartman Longman & Todd, 1965.

Villanueva, Federico G. *Psalms 1–72: A Commentary.* ABCS. Carlisle, UK: Langham Global Library, 2016.

Waltke, Bruce K., and Michael P. O'Connor. *An Introduction to Biblical Hebrew Syntax.* Winona Lake, IN: Eisenbrauns, 1990.

Webb, Barry G. *Five Festal Garments: Christian Reflections on the Song of Songs, Ruth, Lamentations, Ecclesiastes, Esther.* NSBT. Leicester, UK: Apollos, 2000.

———. *The Message of Isaiah.* Leicester, UK: InterVarsity Press, 1996.

Wells, Samuel, and George R. Sumner. *Esther & Daniel.* Brazos Theological Commentary on the Bible. Grand Rapids, MI: Brazos Press, 2013.

Wendt, Reinhard, ed. *An Indian to the Indians?: On the Initial Failure and Posthumous Success of the Missionary Ferdinand Kittel, 1832–1903.* Wiesbaden, Germany: Harrassowitz Verlag, 2006.

Wiesehofer, Josef. "The Achaemenid Empire." In *The Dynamics of Ancient Empires: State Power from Assyria to Byzantium*, edited by Ian Morris and Walter Scheidel. Oxford, UK: Oxford University Press, 2009.

———. *Ancient Persia: From 550 BC to 650 AD.* Translated by Azizeh Azodi. London, England: I. B. Tauris, 2001.

Wintle, Brian C., and Ken Gnanakan. *Ephesians.* ABCS. Singapore: Asia Theological Association, 2006.

Wong, Vivienne. *Grandma in JB Saved Countless Lives during World War II because She Could Speak Japanese*, April 7, 2017. Online: http://www.asiaone.com/malaysia/grandma-jb-saved-countless-lives-during-world-war-ii-because-she-could-speak-japanese.

BIBLIOGRAPHY

Woolf, Nicky. "Christmas Celebrations Banned in Somalia, Tajikistan and Brunei." *The Guardian*, December 23, 2015.

Yamauchi, Edwin M. *Persia and the Bible*. Grand Rapids, MI: Baker Book House, 1996.

Yarshater, Ehsan, ed. *Encyclopedia Iranica*. New York, 1996. Online: www. iranicaonline.org.

Asia Theological Association
54 Scout Madriñan St. Quezon City 1103, Philippines
Email: ataasia@gmail.com Telefax: (632) 410 0312

OUR MISSION

The Asia Theological Association (ATA) is a body of theological institutions, committed to evangelical faith and scholarship, networking together to serve the Church in equipping the people of God for the mission of the Lord Jesus Christ.

OUR COMMITMENT

The ATA is committed to serving its members in the development of evangelical, biblical theology by strengthening interaction, enhancing scholarship, promoting academic excellence, fostering spiritual and ministerial formation and mobilizing resources to fulfill God's global mission within diverse Asian cultures.

OUR TASK

Affirming our mission and commitment, ATA seeks to:

- **Strengthen** interaction through inter-institutional fellowship and programs, regional and continental activities, faculty and student exchange programs.
- **Enhance** scholarship through consultations, workshops, seminars, publications, and research fellowships.
- **Promote** academic excellence through accreditation standards, faculty and curriculum development.
- **Foster** spiritual and ministerial formation by providing mentor models, encouraging the development of ministerial skills and a Christian ethos.
- **Mobilize** resources through library development, information technology and infra-structural development.

To learn more about ATA, visit www.ataasia.com or Facebook /AsiaTheologicalAssociation

☘ Langham
PARTNERSHIP

Langham Literature, along with its publishing work, is a ministry of Langham Partnership.

Langham Partnership is a global fellowship working in pursuit of the vision God entrusted to its founder John Stott –

> *to facilitate the growth of the church in maturity and Christ-likeness through raising the standards of biblical preaching and teaching.*

Our vision is to see churches in the majority world equipped for mission and growing to maturity in Christ through the ministry of pastors and leaders who believe, teach and live by the Word of God.

Our mission is to strengthen the ministry of the Word of God through:
- nurturing national movements for biblical preaching
- fostering the creation and distribution of evangelical literature
- enhancing evangelical theological education

especially in countries where churches are under-resourced.

Our ministry

Langham Preaching partners with national leaders to nurture indigenous biblical preaching movements for pastors and lay preachers all around the world. With the support of a team of trainers from many countries, a multi-level programme of seminars provides practical training, and is followed by a programme for training local facilitators. Local preachers' groups and national and regional networks ensure continuity and ongoing development, seeking to build vigorous movements committed to Bible exposition.

Langham Literature provides majority world preachers, scholars and seminary libraries with evangelical books and electronic resources through publishing and distribution, grants and discounts. The programme also fosters the creation of indigenous evangelical books in many languages, through writer's grants, strengthening local evangelical publishing houses, and investment in major regional literature projects, such as one volume Bible commentaries like *The Africa Bible Commentary* and *The South Asia Bible Commentary*.

Langham Scholars provides financial support for evangelical doctoral students from the majority world so that, when they return home, they may train pastors and other Christian leaders with sound, biblical and theological teaching. This programme equips those who equip others. Langham Scholars also works in partnership with majority world seminaries in strengthening evangelical theological education. A growing number of Langham Scholars study in high quality doctoral programmes in the majority world itself. As well as teaching the next generation of pastors, graduated Langham Scholars exercise significant influence through their writing and leadership.

To learn more about Langham Partnership and the work we do visit **langham.org**

www.ingramcontent.com/pod-product-compliance
Lightning Source LLC
Chambersburg PA
CBHW060353090426
42734CB00011B/2126